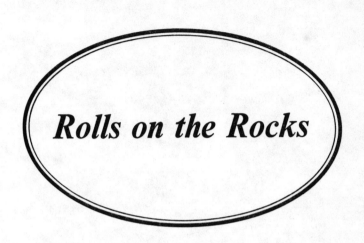

Rolls on the Rocks

ROLLS ON THE ROCKS

The History of Rolls - Royce

Robert Gray

Compton Press · Salisbury

Designed and printed at The Compton Press
Cartoons by J. Tetley

Contents

•

Acknowledgements

In writing this book at full throttle, I have found
some existing source material on Rolls-Royce of
invaluable assistance.

I should like to acknowledge my debt to Harold
Nockold's *The Magic of a Name* (G. T. Foulis,
1938) – a mine of information on Rolls-Royce
history; to Anthony Bird's and Ian Hallows's *The
Rolls-Royce Motor Car* (Batsford, 1964) – a
beautifully-produced, lucid and authoritative work;
to W. A. Robotham's *Silver Ghosts and Silver Dawn*
(Constable, 1970); to Laurence Meynell's *Rolls: Man
of Speed* (Bodley Head, 1953); to Sir Max
Pemberton's *The Life of Sir Henry Royce*
(Hutchinson); and, to put the car in motoring
perspective, Ralph Stein's *The Automobile Book*
(Paul Hamlyn, 1962). Back numbers of the
magazines *Flight* and *Aeroplane* have also proved
useful.

I should like to thank the Rolls-Royce staff, the
many librarians, the technical and financial experts,
and the cuttings department heads at *The Times* and
The Guardian – all of whom helped to direct my
researches.

Without the support of such patient friends as
Juliet Clough, Paul Evans, my publisher Julian Berry
and his wife, Leo Cooper, Carol Bostock who typed
my illegible manuscript, and that industrious
research-assistant my mother, *Rolls on the Rocks*
might have suffered total breakdown.

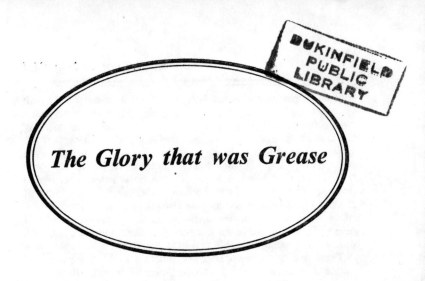

The Glory that was Grease

I

For Rolls-Royce the end came not with a whimper but a bang. Failure to develop one engine, the RB. 211, appeared to be the monstrously inadequate cause for the destruction of Britain's most renowned company. Hindsight may now easily enough discern the danger signals that went unheeded, but to the Prime Minister no less than to the general public (for once in accord with their leader) the first hearing of the news came as 'a bitter shock'. In the Commons on 4 February, 1971 Mr. Frederick Corfield, Minister of Aviation Supply, and his 'shadow' Mr. Wedgwood Benn contrived at least to agree on the 'gravity' of the situation; Mr. Wedgwood Benn would not stick at that but called the collapse of Rolls-Royce 'a major national tragedy'. In the City, where concern for the national honour was less on the lips though perhaps (who can tell) equally on the mind, the *Financial Times* index, which does not even include Rolls-Royce shares, fell 9 points in 24 hours. In Fleet Street the news inspired huge headlines for the better part of a week and cast leader writers into their most portentous frame of mind; *The Times* pronounced this to be 'much the most important company failure in Britain since before the war', nor was there a dissenting voice.

Elsewhere (exact location unspecified) Mrs. Mary Wilson – *The Sunday Times* reported it – was discovered by her returning spouse 'in a state of shock'; she felt it was 'as if we had lost the Rock of Gibraltar'. Most people seemed to agree with her, only differing in choice of metaphor according to taste in sacred cows and (one suspects) daily papers. A defaulting Bank of England, a detonated House of Commons and even, for those who had taken the news especially hard, a demolished Buckingham Palace were all revealed to be much in the public mind.

Obviously something more than a great company had collapsed. In Derby and other Rolls-Royce centres where the end of the RB. 211 contract would cause a possible 20,000 redundancies (not to forget an estimated further 20,000 in companies which supplied Rolls-Royce) the news was indeed enough to cause such dismay. But, making no attempt to minimise the suffering the crash might cause, this alone is not sufficient to explain the general state of shock throughout the country. Seen in the light of cold statistics a further 40,000 unemployed would add only 0·2 per cent to the national unemployment rates. That would put nobody in mind of the Rock of Gibraltar. No, the cause of the widespread public concern lay elsewhere. It lay in a realisation of the national implications of the bankruptcy and also, to a much greater extent, in an awareness of the annihilation of that most intangible, indefinable and valuable of assets – a reputation.

There are two aspects of the crisis that make it a matter of national concern. When the Government announced the nationalisation of Rolls-Royce (see Part III) it explicitly refused to recognise any liabilities regarding the RB. 211 contract. This created fears that Britain's commercial reputation would be seriously damaged and further that there might be some retaliatory action from abroad, perhaps affecting the potential sales of Concorde (the Anglo-French supersonic airliner), or of the Harrier vertical take-off (VTO) to the U.S., and even, in Mr. Wedgwood Benn's somewhat alarmist view, threatening the future of the multi-role aircraft which we are building with the Germans. All these projects are powered by Rolls-Royce engines. It is indeed true that signs very quickly appeared that the Americans would play all their cards in their desperate need to re-negotiate the RB. 211 contract. But talk of national 'honour' being involved is a little overdone for political purposes. It is no use discussing the situation as though it were a moral dilemma presented to a Sunday school class. In such a tough, savagely competitive business as the aircraft industry concepts of honour are a luxury in which no party can afford to indulge – and in their hearts everyone knows this, most of all Lockheed who in March 1968 originally drove the hardest bargain they could with Rolls-Royce, for the £150 million RB. 211 contract.

The other national aspect of the crisis raises deeper and more serious issues. For the problems which Rolls-Royce faced are the problems of Britain in microcosm – though perhaps not so 'micro' when the thousands of millions involved in the aircraft industry are taken into account. This point will be elaborated in Part III, which will attempt to provide a plain man's guide to the Rolls-Royce collapse, but in the meantime a letter from Mr. Anthony Meyer M.P. to *The Times*, published on 10 February, puts the matter with eloquent simplicity: 'There appear to be three possibilities facing Rolls-Royce: to go down the drain, to be taken over by the Americans, or to merge with a European partner. Are not these the possibilities facing Britain?' That is certainly true of advanced technology projects at least: the Rolls-Royce failure is the latest link in a whole chain of evidence, stretching back to the cancellation of Blue Streak, that Britain by herself simply does not have the resources necessary to meet their cost.

For most people, however, the end of Rolls-Royce was a shock because it meant the ruin of a reputation and the shattering of a symbol. Rolls-Royce! Does not the very name suggest the ultimate in reliability and excellence? Indeed, it has passed into the language as a synonym for these qualities; we hear of 'the Rolls-Royce' of bicycles, washing machines, carpet sweepers, cookers, anything. In America the word has even been applied by appreciative, or contrite, husbands to their wives – 'she's a regular Rolls-Roycer'. (That this was a compliment may be safely presumed). Most satisfying of all, everyone understands not only the connotations of the word but also that it was a peculiarly *British* symbol, in some vague way bound up with former British glories. The Empire had gone but we still had Rolls-Royce.

There are those who deride such nostalgia as sentimental, even harmful in that its indulgence prevents us from facing the stern realities of the present, but it surely is not difficult to find some aspects of that past more attractive than the present? Computer processing, business efficiency, managerial science, personnel psychology, and the whole dreary jargon-apparatus of the 'white hot technological revolution' may all be necessary to our national survival but necessity never made anything attractive. The irony of Rolls-Royce's position was that although they were, or were supposed to be, the country's leading exponents of such unlovely contemporary skills, their reputation undoubtedly appealed to and derived from the romantic view of the past. Indeed, it has been argued that this schizophrenic image contributed to their troubles, that the legend of their reputation made them over-confident of their technical abilities, whilst preventing needed changes in the policies and structure of the firm.

Such a reputation as this is not plonked down amongst us fully formed; rather it is an organic growth, the development of which is tied up with many other histories and which draws its strength from many sources. Its heart, of course, has always been the incredibly high engineering expertise and standards which Rolls-Royce have sustained continuously from their earliest days.

To a really astounding degree these standards and skills stem back to one man. 'That would not do for Henry Royce' is still the most damning and final criticism in the Rolls-Royce Derby works. But round him and about them cluster a myriad of achievements and incidents, some great, some trivial, some statistical, some anecdotal, but all cells of the organism, parts of the legend. And this legend was extremely valuable and important. It is true, as Mr. Powell points out, that the technical skills remain but the 'amour propre' that was Rolls-Royce's is not

easily engendered. Any employee would feel more impelled to
stretch his skills for Rolls-Royce than for (say) the British Gas-
Turbine Corporation. A Rolls by any other name does not smell
as sweet.

Since the fatal 4 February – the day Rolls-Royce officially
announced their bankruptcy – there have been hundreds of
articles dissecting Rolls-Royce's putrefying corpse (though there
have been a few faint whispers of a nationalised resurrection).
The Rolls-Royce legend has been excoriated by the very papers
that were prostrate before it in March 1968. Hardly anyone
looked back on the many days of glory or paused to consider
how much the country has owed Rolls-Royce. We should not
allow ourselves to forget the great achievements of the company
or the men who made possible the superb Silver Ghost, the
Schneider Trophy triumphs or the Merlin-powered Spitfires
which helped keep Hitler at bay in the dangerous days of 1940.
It is only by exploring such memories, by tracing the legend back
to its extraordinary originator, that one can understand why the
news of the company's demise hit ordinary people, who know
nothing and care less about the glories of technology, with such
a stunning blow. And so, ignoring for the moment the conversa-
tions of Prime Minister and President on the transatlantic hot-line,
the wrangles of the Cabinet, the loans of bankers, the sorrows
of stockbrokers, the anger of Lockheed and even the gloom
at Derby, let us go back (it is a direct route) to the day, 1 April
1904, when the Rolls-Royce legend began, the day when Henry
Royce drove his first car, never run before, the sixteen miles from
his works in Cook Street, Manchester, to his home at Knutsford
in Cheshire. The legend being what it is, it seems superfluous to
add that the car started immediately, performed perfectly and
gave its owner-designer a trouble-free first journey.

II

Actually the legend got off to a somewhat doubtful start.
Although that first run took place on 1 April 1904 the Royce
publicists announced it as the 31 March. The state of British
humour and the public's view of motoring both being at a somewhat low ebb at that time, it was thought wise to avoid the taunts
that might be attracted by an April Fool's Day début. Moreover,
the story suffers marginally from the claim of one of Royce's
apprentices, Haldenby, who wrote in *The Times* Aviation Supple-
ment of September 1954: 'I drove the first car out for the first
time on 1 April 1904.' Haldenby's syntax, though, still leaves
room for Royce having been the original driver. What is quite
unthinkable, however, is the impression left by some Rolls-
Royce devotees that the engine began its life with the first turn
of the starting handle on that occasion. Like all Royce engines it

would have been thoroughly tested on the bench previously.

This first car – or chassis more properly – was a 2-cylinder 10 h.p. model. So powerful are the associations of the name that a Rolls-Royce, or even a Royce, of such lowly rating almost seems like a contradiction in terms, even though, as we shall see, it was in the circumstances one of the most remarkable of all Royce's achievements.

And 1904! A German Jew who lived in Vienna, Siegfried Marcus, had produced a petrol-engined car as far back as 1865; in the 1930s the Nazis' dedication to the primacy of all things Teutonic led them to seek to destroy it. By 1888 Benz had sold some of his cars in Paris, the first small deals in what was to become one of the twentieth century's staple trades. To those sensitive on such matters (and in Britain there are many) it comes as a shock to find that the aristocratic Rolls-Royce, which assumes an impeccable pedigree in the casual way most of us put on a mackintosh, was in fact comparatively (even by national standards) an *arriviste* on the motoring scene. But then the whole country has lagged ludicrously behind in motor car development. At first sight this seems surprising: England had led the industrial revolution and the railway age; thanks to Telford and Macadam she had – at least by the standards of that time – good roads; most important, especially to those who claim that technical development proceeds according to economic demand, she had a prosperous upper middle class only too well able to indulge in the expensive excitements offered by the motoring age. None of these factors, however, could surmount the insuperable obstacle of the 1865 Locomotives Act and the notorious insistence on the car being preceded by a bearer of a red flag.

To understand the cause of this monstrous legislation it is necessary to go briefly back to the 1820s and 1830s which had seen a false dawn of the self-propelled road vehicle's age. For in these years all variety of weird steam contraptions proliferated: one carriage even had steam-powered 'legs', complete with joints, to help it mount steep hills. In London and in parts of the country there were steam bus services, although, with the dangers from faulty steering, hopeless brakes and, most hazardous of all, bursting boilers, such travelling made courage a more indispensable prerequisite than money for the fare.

Of course these vehicles were unpopular – they belched soot, scattered sparks and deafened all and sundry. Notwithstanding this, steam carriages had great potential, as is demonstrated by the fact that in the early twentieth century they competed equally with – and in America indeed outsold – petrol cars; in 1906 a steam car held the world speed record (121 m.p.h.) and in the States they were produced up to the beginning of the Second World War. But back in the early nineteenth century they had far more formidable enemies than the powerless and inarticulate resentment they aroused in ordinary people. These were the railway and coaching interests. The railway companies were well-represented by their directors in the House of Commons, and the anti-steam car brigade was equally in control of the counties. The result was a succession of ever-steepening tolls and the 1865 and other Acts which drove almost all self-propelled vehicles off the road. Here are some of the provisions of that legislation.

1. At least three persons had to be employed to drive a self-propelled vehicle.
2. While the vehicle was in motion one of these passengers was required to precede the vehicle on foot by at least 20 yards.
3. Drivers had to give way to all other traffic, which was empowered to stop self-propelled vehicles by simply raising a hand.
4. The speed limit was 4 m.p.h., or 2 m.p.h. in towns and villages.
5. There was a licence fee of £10 *per county* in which the vehicle was used.

In the light of such a law it is easy to forgive English engineers for being backward motor manufacturers. While the motor car began to make headway in France throughout the 1890s, and the de Dion and Panhard et Levassor companies established its basic design, in England the pioneers of motoring were concentrating on getting the English law altered. Such enthusiasts as the Hon. Charles Rolls deliberately flaunted the traffic acts in the hope of inviting a prosecution which would expose their iniquities; but all to no avail: the English respect for a title proved stronger than their respect for the sanctity of the law so that Rolls at least motored unmolested. Others, of lowlier origin, were not so fortunate and one offender found himself facing the unanswerable prosecution charge that since the policeman caught him he must have been breaking the limit. Eventually, however, reason prevailed and in 1896 the speed limit was boldly raised to 12 m.p.h. There followed the celebratory and celebrated first London to Brighton run, the joy of the occasion being marred only by the Earl of Winchelsea's failure to tear asunder the symbolic red flag without resort to his penknife. So Britain reluctantly reached the motoring age and the first British makes of car, with such famous names as Lanchester, Wolseley (designed by Austin), Napier and Sunbeam among them, appeared with their earliest models. Meanwhile, Henry Royce, the Crown Prince, was making electric cranes.

III

In 1863 Henry Royce was born, poor, into an era and country in which a great part of the moneyed classes took to the comforting view that poverty was a crime of which the poor were unpardonably and unforgiveably guilty. A little moral fibre, a degree of industry, a hassock-load of prayer, above all, abstention from drink, would soon bring comfort, honour and riches into the humblest home, or if not, at least the glowing consciousness of duty well done.

Needless to say, the reception by the middle classes of such rude mechanicals as successfully followed their teachings did not always accord with the sincerity with which they undoubtedly believed their morality; like all propertied classes they preferred their social inferiors to be conspicuous for honest endeavour rather than for definite achievement.

Four years before Royce's birth, in 1859, Samuel Smiles had published his 'Self-Help' which rapidly became one of the standard articles of the Victorian faith. Never did preceptor have a more ardent exemplar of his doctrines than Henry Royce. Indeed, the great mechanic's whole career might have been created to illustrate, to those who believed in a Creator, the fundamental wisdom and justice of the social order. Such people never mind the odd bit of suffering in others if it proves their point, and Henry Royce had no easy youth. Industry, thrift, dedication, self-discipline, sense of duty, however, he had them all and they duly earned their reward. But of course it helped to have mechanical genius as well.

Royce's first years were spent at Alwalton in Lincolnshire, where his father was a miller. The story goes that the two-year-old boy became so fascinated by the wheels of the mill that he fell into the mill-race and was only saved in the nick of time by his father. That is the only action of Royce senior's which posterity has observed with favour; indeed, for no very compelling reason most un-Rolls-Royce words like 'unsatisfactory', 'unstable', and 'unreliable' have clung to his non-silver ghost. Certainly he was not a material success. Milling is traditionally a remunerative occupation, yet somehow (it is vaguely suggested somewhere by an attempt to instal steam machinery) his job in Lincolnshire evaporated, and in 1867 he took two of his five children with him to London, where shortly afterwards he died.

Henry Royce was thus forced, like so many London children of that period, to provide for his own needs. There could be no question of proper education. He continued unconsciously to play his classic role of self-made man by becoming a newspaper boy. He was nine years old, with one year's schooling behind him; this, with another between eleven and twelve, seems to have been the sum of his formal education. There must have seemed so little hope of success for him that even dreaming of it would have appeared presumptuous. For the next five years life was simply a quest for the next meal; nothing could have been further from the future glamour of Rolls-Royce. Then, when he was fourteen, an aunt, relic perhaps of the more prosperous Royce past, took on a commitment of £20 a year for him to be

apprenticed to the Great Northern Railway Works at Peterborough. Did she recognise, or hear of, his latent mechanical
talent, or was her happy choice just good fortune? Anyway, it
removed him from the hopeless slough of London and introduced
him to a world where his bent could become manifest. He was in
fact doubly fortunate for not only could he work on the great
locomotives but also he was boarded with a man who possessed
a lathe and was prepared to spend time teaching Royce how to
use it and other tools. This was, as far as is known, the only
instruction Royce ever received in the mechanical skills for
which he became pre-eminent. His ability to use hand tools with
as great a precision as machines doing the same task was to
amaze associates in later years.

He had been at Peterborough for three years when misfortune
struck again: his aunt ran short of money and his apprenticeship
necessarily ended. It is intriguing to speculate what he might
have achieved in railway engineering, had the fates willed. But
in 1880 all Royce knew was that he was out of money and in
need of a job at a time when the economy was depressed for the
first time in years. From Peterborough he set out on foot to the
north, searching without success for work. Eventually he had
what he was obliged to regard as the good fortune to land a job
in an armaments factory at Leeds. The pay – eleven shillings
(55p) for a 54-hour week. Yet he found time to become fascinated
in a subject that must have seemed an odd choice for an un-
educated teenager – electricity, then beginning to be put to
practical use for the first time.

Electricity was to 'make' Royce, but that was still a long way
ahead; at Leeds its study was just a hobby pursued with ever-
increasing enthusiasm. Soon, though, he saw his chance. The
London Electric Light and Power Company, one of the first in
the field, advertised for a tester and Royce applied. Although
completely unqualified, he landed the job, such is the advantage of
applying oneself to a pioneer science. Not that the Company
were anything but extremely fortunate to get him, as they soon
recognised. The position gave him the opportunity to attend night
classes at the City and Guilds Technical College, and at the
Polytechnic. At the age of nineteen he was appointed chief electrical engineer to the scheme for the electric lighting of the streets
of Liverpool. He was also, as he later liked to recall, indirectly
concerned with the theatre in his new office. One of the great
problems of early electricity was that the extinguishing of one
light would cause the dynamo to race and put out the remaining
bulbs. Royce was concerned to see that this did not happen
and kept the lights shining equally through many theatre per-
formances.

Despite the ability with which Royce coped with these and
other difficulties, the company went bust and again he was
unemployed. But by now Royce had been shrewd enough to

save £20 and, shrewder still, had made a friend, A. E. Claremont, with £50. In 1884 men and money coalesced to form 'F. H. Royce & Company' of Cook Street, Manchester, which company would seek to exploit its namesake's electrical skills. When the relative financial contributions of the two partners are considered the name of the new company is eloquent testimony to Royce's ability and force of personality. He was still only twenty-one.

There was no immediate success, no startling invention that rocked the world. Royce's talent did not, as we shall see, lend itself to explosively original concepts. The new company began by making electric light filaments and soon Royce was selling an electric bell set, an exciting gadget in those days. It retailed at one shilling and sixpence (7½p) and sold well; at that price it had to, if there were to be any profit. Then Royce set about improving existing dynamos, producing a type the reliability and longevity of which gradually made it popular for lighting factories and ships.

All the while the business of the little company was slowly mounting and in 1894 it assumed the rather grandiloquent title of 'Royce, Ltd., Electrical & Mechanical Engineers, & Manufacturers of Dynamos, Motors & kindred articles'. The 'kindred articles' soon included electric cranes which proved to be the greatest commercial success thus far. Like all Royce articles they were superbly engineered and unbreakable even in the hands of the most ruthless contractors. They were also perfectly suited to the needs of the market, falling between the unwieldy steam cranes and the only previous alternative, manpower. In October 1897 there were orders worth £6,000; in March 1898 £9,000, and in February 1899 £20,000. In order to enable the company to meet this demand capital was increased to £30,000. It was an impressive figure compared with the £70 of fifteen years before.

Then suddenly the demand for cranes began to fall off. Royce's cranes were good but they were expensive, his motto being that 'the quality remains after the price has been forgotten'. When new and cheaper types were imported from America and Germany anxious friends begged him to relax his standards a little so as to remain competitive. His reaction to such suggestions is most illuminating; he returned an uncompromising, even an arrogant, refusal to do anything of the sort. If people didn't want the best cranes he could produce that provided no cause for making bad cranes. There would always be a demand for excellence. This was, and is, far from being good commercial sense, however admirable in other respects, but here, seventy years ago, is a Rolls-Royce attitude utterly recognisable to us. The tradition preceded the company even as it was to survive its originator. Royce had the good fortune, however, to find his métier in a product, motor cars, where purchasers are not guided by cold, rational, objective, economic arguments. For example, nobody could prove that a modern Rolls-Royce is

worth £10,000 more than a large Ford; indeed, it would be far
easier to prove that the difference in price is ridiculous. This
however, is beside the point. For many people cars are not susceptible to nice calculations of value; they are status-symbols,
fantasy-fulfilments, girl-catchers, which is why there have always
been purchasers willing to pay a great deal more money for only
a small increase in quality. By no stretch of the imagination,
though, could these considerations be said to apply to cranes, and
so it seemed in 1903 that Royce's was a declining company, the
victim of its originator's unrealistic attachment to the highest
standards. Royce needed a new line and a skilful publicist to
advertise his dedication to quality. Both were forthcoming.

IV

Although in 1900 Royce had been concerned with the design of a
dynamo for an electric car, his enthusiasm for the motor age
seems to have been surprisingly slow in kindling. Obviously this
was partly a matter of economics, but it still seems odd that
before 1903 there should have been no report of any interest
being displayed by the greatest mechanic of the day in the most
exciting new mechanical invention. But when the bug did bite it
bit hard. In that year Royce, still affluent from the former sales
of his dynamo, bought a car, a 10 h.p. Decauville.

It is reported that so impatient did he become with this car's
faults and bad design that in exasperation he set about producing
his own model. This is perfectly true; like most early cars the
Decauville was noisy and it vibrated abominably. Early cars had
no adequate throttle control and so the engines raced when
stationary, a major cause of their unpopularity with passers-by.
But in their authoritative work, *The Rolls-Royce Motor Car*,
Anthony Bird and Ian Hallows do much to salvage the French
car's reputation, claiming that it had some features (notably an
'extremely well-designed, and quiet, live axle') which were
decidedly advanced for the time. Moreover it was thoroughly
reliable as had been proved at the Crystal Palace in 1900 when a
Decauville had run for 1,000 miles non-stop. In the case of Royce's
model it is hard to believe such reliability was not affected by
the regularity with which he dismembered it, but he paid it the
sincerest form of flattery by incorporating some parts of the
Decauville design into his own first cars. But if Royce could
return today and buy the latest Rolls-Royce he would immediately set about improving it. For all the Decauville virtues it
was not surprising that such a fanatically perfectionist mechanic
found faults that were intolerable to him. Principally he determined that in his own cars he would attempt to overcome the
noise problem. Throughout the winter of 1903–4 he worked day
and night with two apprentices to get the first Royce finished.

The Royce method of work had already been long established. He never made any claim to be a brilliant inventor, the sort of man who astonishes an era by a sudden, almost intuitive, burst of thought. His lack of education meant that he knew little of mathematics and he thus lacked the equipment for conceptual thought. His approach to mechanics therefore began and ended with practical experiment. 'There's no safe way of judging anything except by experiment' was his creed. All experiments brought information, especially, he considered, the unsuccessful ones. Once he had seen why a machine went wrong it was comparatively an easy matter for someone of his gifts to correct the fault. He sought to make his cars go wrong so that he could prevent the fault occurring again. No sooner had he designed a car than he would turn his ingenuity towards testing it, to destruction if possible. His first engine was connected to a dynamo in order to assess the power output. His first car would often be attached to a huge block of granite to assess its performance under a heavy load.

Soon he was creating more sophisticated and fiendish devices, including a bumping machine which could concentrate into a few hours thousands of miles of running over the worst terrain. These methods point to the essence of his talent, which was to bring whatever piece of machinery he studied to such a peak of perfection in every tiny detail that it could no longer properly be called the same machinery. He had done this with dynamos and cranes, he was doing it with cars, and he would do it again with aero-engines. In this unrelenting pursuit of excellence nothing was too unimportant for him to ignore until it was perfect. One who knew him from his Leeds days, Arthur Wormald, (later Works Manager of Rolls-Royce at Derby) summed up Royce's early work with motor cars as follows:

> I do not think that Sir Henry did anything of a revolutionary nature in his work on motor cars in the early days. He did, however, do much important development work and a considerable amount of re-designing of existing devices and apparatus, so that his motor cars were far and away better than anyone else's motor cars.
>
> I cannot say that there was any outstanding original invention incorporated in the 10 h.p. two cylinder cars, but I can say that every unit of that car was of a better and sounder design than was to be found in contemporary makes. He paid great attention to the smallest detail and the result of his personal consideration to every little thing resulted in the whole assembly being of a very high standard of perfection.
>
> It is rather to Sir Henry's thoroughness and unending attention to even the smallest detail than to any revolutionary invention that his products have the superlative qualities which we all know so well.
>
> The overhead valve was not an innovation of Sir Henry's; others had it but Sir Henry's method of applying it was years ahead of the rest.
>
> In the same way Sir Henry was not the first to adopt shaft drive

in place of chains, but here again his shaft drive cut out many weaknesses in the then existing designs.

From what has been said of Royce's approach to his work it follows that he could only succeed by dint of unflagging industry. There was always a new design to be experimented with or a new part to be tested: his achievements were built from an infinite number of separate particles. Luckily Royce was endowed from the beginning with a totally obsessional involvement in his work; it permeated his every fibre. Maybe this obsession stemmed from his childhood experiences; maybe it was that in the early days at Cook Street, poverty had forced him to live on the job all round the clock for want of any alternative board. More likely his mind was so devoted to his work that he just had no desire for any release from it. Early associates recall him poring in a trance-like state over his task, totally oblivious of the noise and activity that hummed around him. For months on end he would work a twenty-hour day, falling asleep over his bench. Even getting him to eat required considerable strategic skill on the part of his fellows; apprentices would be detailed to take him bread and milk at opportune moments.

Nothing in these habits and nothing in Royce's own background of struggle was calculated to make him an easy man to work with or at all an indulgent employer. Dignitaries who met the elusive Royce late in his life, when his personality had doubtless benefited from his triumphs, speak of his charm and kindness, but at this stage these qualities, if they existed, were often severely repressed. An employee of Royce's (Evernden) recalled: 'I not only admired him, I was one of the few people who were genuinely fond of him . . . Henry Royce ruled the lives of the people around him, claimed them body and soul, even when they were asleep.' Any suggestion of skimping or any attempt to pass off shoddy workmanship instantly aroused his ire and he would pounce with the ferocity of an Inquisitor on an Anabaptist.

> 'When angered he could be rough tongued' Bird and Hallows confess: 'Indeed, to be blunt his benign and rather sensitive face was not matched by any corresponding mildness of expression and his outbursts of profanity were startling in one so retiring by nature.'

At the same time he could not tolerate the meek – 'I made him swear' he is said to have commented with satisfaction after an exchange with some weaker spirit.

In nearly every respect his treatment of employees broke any rule a personnel manager could name. One of his ploys was to point to a half-finished chassis at five to one on a Saturday morning (work officially stopped at lunchtime) and say 'I'm going home in that one'. So the rest of the day was spent in making it ready. The working week for his apprentices frequently mounted to a hundred hours, for which they received the meagre reward of five shillings (25p). 'You haven't earned it,' he would comment as they took their wages. Ironically intended or not, the effect of such treatment on a modern trade unionist can well enough be imagined. There is no doubt where Royce would have stood in the current industrial battles. Almost at the end of his life, in 1931, he wrote to an acquaintance:

'This year has been particularly bad owing to the general lack of orders and the still lower prices. Most of England is in the same bad way, and I cannot see any hope. . . . It is to be hoped that the trade unions will see it is impossible to compete, and that we cannot have a high standard of wage on a short day, and heavy taxes.'

And yet, despite these views and the intolerable conditions they imposed, most of Royce's apprentices worshipped him for his skill. It was hard to work with him, but many good men and true found it harder still to leave him. Themselves fascinated by mechanics, they could not throw away the opportunity of working with a master-talent. So we find that many of Royce's assistants in those early days stayed on, later to become leading names in Rolls-Royce. Haldenby and Platford, the two apprentices who helped Royce on his original car, became respectively General Manager and Chief Tester. Wormald, as already mentioned, became Works Manager. De Looze, in charge of finance at Royce's since 1893, became the first company secretary of Rolls-Royce. E. W. Hives, who joined in 1908 to supervise experimental work, earned a peerage and became Joint Managing Director of Rolls-Royce together with A. G. Elliott, whose association with the company dated from 1912. These men were the vital links in the chain which bound the standards of Henry Royce to the modern company.

Such were the conditions under which the first cars were built. It must be remembered that the electrical side of the business was still continuing at Cook Street so that an outsider visiting the works would have had difficulty in distinguishing the bits and pieces of the cars, (nearly all of which were manufactured on the spot by Royce) from the electrical and crane equipment. Once there was a hold-up because the front axle was discovered to be marginally out of line. An assistant who tried to rectify the error in haphazard fashion received a blistering rebuke and, notwithstanding the delay involved, the axle was altogether discarded.

This first car, like its successors, was revolutionary not in any single part, but in the excellence of the whole. None the less, points of especial notice were the battery and coil ignition system (Royce's electrical background was useful here), an improved carburettor and a well designed exhaust system fitted with a huge silencer. The engine had two cylinders and drove the rear wheels through a cone clutch and three speed gearbox. Maximum speed was about thirty m.p.h. and the car weighed $14\frac{1}{2}$ cwt. What people

immediately noticed was its silence, a Rolls-Royce tradition from
the very beginning. In fact the car was in every way a worthy
ancestor of the line that derived from it. But what chance was
there of it coming before the public eye?

Royce made three of these 10 h.p. prototypes; unfortunately
none now survives. The first he kept for his own use, the second
was taken by his partner, Claremont, and had an unfortunate
history of breakdowns, perhaps caused by Royce's continuous
modifications. Poor Claremont was obliged to be followed about
by a hansom cab so that he could continue his journey even when
the car could not. He even had a notice printed – 'If this car
breaks down please don't ask a lot of silly questions' – to quell
humourists who took advantage of his embarrassments. The
third car, fortunately, was more reliable and became the property
of Mr. Henry Edmunds, who was an eminent figure in motoring
circles, and had recently been made a director of Royce's. This
was a shrewd move, for one of Henry Edmunds's friends was the
Hon. Charles Rolls.

V

At Derby they still talk of 'Royce's', not 'Rolls-Royce'. This
implied judgment may be a just enough comment on the res-
pective contributions of the two men to the achievements of the
firm which bears their names, although it is doubtful if Royce,
for all his ability, could have made good without the assistance
and the outlets which Rolls was able to provide. Moreover, the
implication of the 'Royce's' tradition, that Rolls was an aristocratic booby who had the good fortune to stumble into a genius,
is most unfair. Rolls was a very considerable mechanic (Haldenby, who worked under both Rolls and Royce, gives a glowing
account of Rolls's ability) and was in every way well qualified to
appreciate the extent of the unknown Royce's talent. Of how
many Etonians of the 1880s and '90s – or indeed today – could
that be said? Indeed, at Eton Rolls had incurred the scorn of his
contemporaries for so far forgetting his social position as to
interest himself in engineering; but his aristocratic indifference to
their opinions combined with his devotion to and ability in his
chosen pursuits proved more than a match for the infantile
contumely of his schoolfellows.

While it is difficult to compare Rolls's early career with that of
Royce without registering a retrospective protest against the
iniquitous and chasmic gulf which separated the two Nations, it
should be remembered that privilege provides temptations as
insidious if more alluring than those of poverty, and that Charles
Rolls did not succumb.

He was born in 1877, the third son of Lord Llangattock, and
during the years of Royce's struggles enjoyed a thoroughly com-

fortable childhood at his family's large country house in Monmouthshire. From the very beginning he showed himself fascinated by all things mechanical. And by a curious coincidence one of his earliest hobbies was, like Royce's, electricity. Once he had even gone to the lengths of lugging a dynamo back to Eton with him, which alarmed the authorities a good deal. A local shopkeeper also remembered him as a boy buying an electric bell; could it possibly have been one of Royce's?

Rolls's adult life was a succession of locomotive crazes, to such an extent that one is irresistibly reminded of his famous contemporary, Mr. Toad. But the comparison is unjust, for there was never anything dilettante or ridiculous about Rolls when in the grip of an enthusiasm, and he shared neither that other gentleman's immodesty nor his truculence. His first craze was cycling and when at Cambridge he designed and built a 'quadruplet', a monstrous but magnificent bicycle for four. Already, however, he had been to France and discovered the motor car, beside which cycling soon seemed to provide small excitement. Rolls was the first undergraduate to have a car at Cambridge, a privilege which at once brought censure and reprieve: 'I often *nearly* got into a row for arriving back late at night after a breakdown; but I squared numerous venerable dons by taking them out in the car. A good many of these runs, however, ended in pushing the car home with the assistance of my venerable passengers who often thus presented a very comic picture, arrayed, as they frequently were, in caps and gowns.'

Notwithstanding these distractions he managed to acquire an excellent mechanics degree and, after leaving Cambridge, became one of the most famous English motor enthusiasts, travelling widely on the Continent both to inspect new cars and to compete in races. In 1900 he won the Thousand Mile Reliability Trial, driving a 12 h.p. Panhard, and three years later he broke the world speed record by doing 93 m.p.h. in a 70 h.p. Mors.

In 1902, seeking to put his experience and his fame to profitable use, he set up a business in Conduit Street, London W.1., still the main Rolls-Royce showrooms, where, under the name C. S. Rolls & Co. he sold and repaired cars, his workshops being at Lillie Hall, Earls Court. A remark in a letter he wrote at the end of 1903 – 'repairs doing *v.* well, sales bad' – tellingly suggests the difficulties facing a motor dealer at that time and Rolls was always on the look out for a thoroughly reliable make of car to sell. Meanwhile, however, the business prospered so that in 1904 he invited Claude Johnson, destined to be a vital figure in Rolls-Royce history, to join him as a partner. Then, in March of that year, came the following letter:

My dear Rolls,
I have pleasure in enclosing you photographs and specification of the Royce car which I think you will agree with me looks very

promising. I have written them asking if they can make an early
appointment to meet you in London; and also whether they can
arrange to send up a car for your inspection and trial. The point that
impressed me most, however, is this. The people have worked out
their designs in their own office and knowing as I do the skill of Mr.
Royce as a practical mechanical engineer, I feel one is very safe in
taking up any work his firm may produce.

Trusting this matter may lead to business to our mutual interest in
the future, believe me,

Yours faithfully,

Henry Edmunds

Edmunds's tribute to Royce was nothing more than the truth
but, had he known of Edmunds's shareholding and directorship
in Royce's, Rolls may have taken it with a pinch of salt. At any
rate he made no immediate move and Edmunds warned Royce of
Rolls's inveterate prejudice against 2-cylinder cars. But he persisted with his matchmaking and eventually earned himself the
soubriquet of 'godfather' to Rolls-Royce by overcoming Rolls's
reluctance to risk wasting a day in Manchester. On the train
going north, Rolls spoke to Edmunds about his business.
Hitherto he had sold chiefly French cars, Panhards and Minervas.
'The cars I sold were, I believe, the best that could be got at the
time; but somehow I always had a feeling that I would prefer to
be selling English instead of foreign goods. In addition I could
distinctly notice a growing desire on the part of my clients to
purchase English-made ones . . . yet I could not come across any
English-made car that I really liked . . . The majority of English
manufacturers at that time all seemed to suffer from the same
thing, what I might call sheer pigheadedness, that is to say they
had a deep-rooted objection to copying the foreigner who had
had many years more experience.' Edmunds recounts how Rolls
told him that it was his ambition to have a motor car connected
with his name so that in future it would be a household word,
just as much as 'Broadwood' or 'Steinway' in connection with
pianos. These ambitions disclosed, Rolls stepped off the train at
Manchester to meet Royce.

There can be no surprises about the results of this encounter.
The two men, with Edmunds as recording angel, lunched at the
Grand Central. 'I think both men took to each other at first sight
and they eagerly discussed the prospects and requirements of the
automobile industry.' Rolls must have been delighted to find that
Royce's ideals of quietness and reliability in cars so exactly
matched the demands of his customers. His good impressions
were more than confirmed when he drove Royce's car. The prejudice against two cylinders was instantly removed. Rolls-Royce
was born.

Or rather conceived. For the moment the two men contented
themselves with an agreement (December 1904) between their
separate companies rather than a merger. Rolls continued to sell

other makes of car but he would market Royce's under the joint name Rolls-Royce. The needs and abilities of the two men were ideally complementary. Rolls received what were effectively sole rights to the products of probably the most skilled mechanic in the world and in turn was able, by dint of his social position and aristocratic contacts, to give Royce access to and make him known in a market which he could not otherwise have reached from his works in Cook Street; a market, moreover, which was tailor-made for Royce's obsessive perfectionism to exploit. In addition – and Royce could not have appreciated in 1904 just how important this would be – the association with Rolls brought him into contact with Claude Johnson ('C.J.' in Rolls-Royce history) an inspired publicist, an organisational genius and the man who forged Royce's obsession with standards into the Rolls-Royce legend.

Johnson has been called 'the hyphen between Rolls and Royce' but the title does him less than justice.

VI

By the agreement of December 1904 Royce undertook to provide Rolls with four types of chassis:

  i A 10 h.p. 2 cylinder to sell at £395
 ii A 15 h.p. 3 cylinder to sell at £500
iii A 20 h.p. 4 cylinder to sell at £650
 iv A 30 h.p. 6 cylinder to sell at £890

Now Royce really had work on his hands; three new models and the 10 h.p. all to be produced simultaneously. A photograph of the Cook Street works taken at the time shows a jumble of cars scattered pell-mell in various stages of completion. By contemporary standards production was on a tiny scale – altogether only 16 Tens, 6 Fifteens, 40 Twenties and 37 Thirties. Of this total only six are known to have survived, three Tens and one of each of the others. None of the three prototype Tens now exist although one was used by the Rolls-Royce works at Derby to take parcels to the station until the 1930s. Then, like so many Rolls-Royce prototypes, it was ruthlessly destroyed.

The Tens had a notable success at the 1904 Paris Show, winning a gold medal. *Motor News* struck out with timid temerity: 'I am rarely tempted into the realms of prophecy but I venture the opinion that Messrs. Royce and Company will make a high reputation for themselves with their all British cars.' The writer was on sure ground; some sixty years later a surviving Ten, the oldest Rolls-Royce in the world, was taking the London to Brighton run in its stride, averaging 11 m.p.h. and doing 14 miles to the gallon. *Country Life* committed itself unhesitatingly to ecstasy over the Paris Show Tens but could not withhold from its readers a nagging anxiety: 'It (the 10 h.p.) was, in a single word, a revelation . . . never before have I been in a car which made so little noise, vibrated so little, ran so smoothly or could be turned about so easily and readily in a maze of traffic. Indeed, the conclusion I reached then and there was that the car was too silent and ghost-like to be safe. That the engine could be set running while the car was at rest without any noise or vibration perceptible to the occupants of the car was good; that the car in motion should overtake numerous wayfarers without their giving any indication of their having heard it, so that the horn had frequently to be called into use, was almost carrying excellence too far.'

Despite this praise of the Ten it is noteworthy that the Twenties and Thirties proved the best sellers of these early Rolls-Royces. This was in accord with contemporary fashions which favoured big six cylinder models. Brooke, Napier, Sunbeam and Spyker all specialised in this type of car, and, notwithstanding the noise they made, their performance was impressive, most of them being capable of 60 to 70 m.p.h. As yet no Rolls-Royce could match them in speed, for although the Thirty was the direct ancestor of the Silver Ghost, a lot of intensive Royce work lay between the two. Connoisseurs find the Twenty the most remarkable of the first production cars and we shall be hearing more of its achievements. Especially difficult for us to believe is that the Rolls-Royces were not extraordinarily expensive by the standards of the day. A 60 h.p. Mercedes cost about £2,500, and, though that was the highest priced car on the market, there were many others dearer than Rolls-Royces, including what was perhaps the leading British marque, the 6-cylinder Napier, which was to be the Rolls-Royce's most formidable early competitor. The Napier cost £1,050.

In one feature at least the first Rolls-Royces would have been completely recognisable to us – the famous classical-styled radiator. The three prototype cars had not possessed this Rolls-Royce hallmark and there is an account of its origin that casts a somewhat tarnishing light on the glories of its genealogy. A firm called Blackburn and Co. had made a car called the Norfolk with an almost identical radiator, but, the remainder of the car being perhaps less noteworthy than the design of the radiator, had ceased production in order to concentrate on more lucrative ventures. A few workers from Blackburn's, however, deprived of their brainchild, found their way to the rapidly expanding Royce works at Manchester. One does not need to be unduly irreverent to suppose that they passed on the chief glory of their former work to their new master. Certainly, from what we know of Royce's methods, he was ever prepared to adopt, and determined to improve, the inventions of others. The simple nobility of the radiator's design would have had an especial appeal to one who disliked any kind of unnecessary ornament. Indeed, although no man was ever more concerned about the efficient design of machinery, he needed Rolls's persuasion to convince him that some concession to the public taste was necessary in the matter of external finish. Thus the first production models looked a degree smarter than the original prototypes. But it must be emphasised that Rolls-Royce produced only the chassis and not a complete car. Not until 1946 did Rolls-Royce sell cars with a standard body. Before that the bodywork was designed and made by such celebrated coach builders as Mulliner, Barker and Hooper, although the terms of their agreement with Rolls-Royce specified in great detail the limits within which they could operate. Fortunately Royce's work was so perfect that they were nearly always inspired to match his efforts with worthy designs and quality. In fact Royce gave them new opportunities; his chassis provided such a smooth ride that it became easier to make doors that would not jam and coachwork that would not be shaken to bits. Thus the closed car became first a possibility and eventually a normality.

Even four models did not suffice to engage all Royce's working hours in those hectic days. In 1905 the vigilant *Autocar* espionage system uncovered rumours of a new model:

> We hear of a Rolls-Royce landaulette. There is quite an air of mystery about it. From what we can gather it has no chains – in fact no gears at all worth mentioning. Its engine can neither be seen, felt, smelt, nor heard, and it takes up very little more room than a cab without a horse, and will turn in the width of a narrow street. Just how it does all these things we are not at liberty to mention at present, but we hope, in a week or two, to say something a little less vague. There is even a rumour to the effect that there is a prize to be given to the first man who finds the engine, but we give no credence to this.

The fact is that Rolls and Claude Johnson had a dangerous rival in the electric brougham. At the turn of the century it seemed that steam and electric cars had quite as much a future as their petrol-driven counterparts. An electric car was the first to do a mile a minute (in 1899); a steam car the first to do two miles a minute (in 1906). The difficulty with 'electrics' was that the batteries were so heavy and held their charge for so short a time that either their range or their speed had to be strictly limited. But they became popular as run-about town cars, their comparative silence being especially appreciated. Royce was thus set the challenge of producing a car that would combine the advantages of both electric and petrol vehicles. The outcome has always impressed technical devotees (for he designed a shallow, flat engine that fitted under the floor) but unfortunately failed to sell. In 1903 the speed limit had been raised to 20 m.p.h. (at which it officially remained until 1930, such is the alacrity with which British governments adapt to changed conditions), and, making a virtue out of necessity, the publicity for the new model advertised it as the 'Legalimit' because it was expressly designed to reach 20 m.p.h., but no more, whatever the gradient. The first model (price £1,160) was purchased by Lord Northcliffe but even this example failed to inspire the public to emulation and only four Legalimits were ever made. None survives. Clearly righteousness is no use as a sales gambit, particularly in the case of cars. But as the man from Rolls-Royce said, 'even our mistakes are beautifully made'.

VII

Meanwhile Rolls and Johnson had been doing their utmost to publicise the excellence of Royce's other models. At the end of 1904 Rolls arranged to meet H.R.H. the Duke of Connaught, one of Queen Victoria's sons, at Folkestone and he took care to advertise that his faith in the reliability of his 10 h.p. Rolls-Royce exceeded even his fear of the ducal anger by ostentatiously setting off from London on the morning of the encounter. He met the Duke on time, took him on a tour of inspection along the coast and returned to London the same night, a total of 220 miles in one day. Then when the Headmaster of Eton retired Rolls ensured that the present from Old Etonians should be a Rolls-Royce. Whether the headmaster was in fact a motorist is not disclosed, but it was a shrewd way of bringing the car to the notice of the Old Etonians. And at Army Manoeuvres in 1905 there was Rolls with his car again, driving the inspecting generals.

More adventurous was Rolls's 1906 assault in a Twenty on the London/Monte Carlo record time which stood at 37½ hours. His companion was Massac Buist who has left this vivid account of that hectic drive:

> In checking over the provisions after 'C.S.R.' had gone to bed on the eve of the attempt, I discovered that there were two half bottles of champagne and much cold tea. On enquiring the scheme of this, Mr. Rolls explained quite seriously that the champagne was for himself and that the tea was for the rest of us. . . .
>
> In the middle of the night we ran into a driving rain storm, which made the going heavy and greatly increased our difficulties in seeing the road. The car had no latter-day 'all-weather' equipment and I had to thrust the marked route in front of the oil side lamp and try to make out my notes, which 'also ran', the whole book becoming more and more pulp-like. At one level crossing, the gates of which we foreknew would have to be closed at the time we were timed to approach, because an express train would also be due, we had speculated 10 francs on the way down as a tip to the man to be ready to open the gates instantly and momentarily at the sound of our horn – rather a dramatic effect, I had fondly hoped. Because of the storm, however, the wretch assumed we should not turn up, so kept snug in bed. It took us a quarter of an hour to rouse him. Having

got him to open the gates we had to look out for an important dividing of the ways a kilometre or so further on. The driver, however, who was so excited by the needless delay and the heavy going, feeling that all the trouble was for naught, forged ahead furiously. Soon we were unmistakably on the wrong road, having shot past the fork while I was struggling with the map under the feeble flicker of the lamp in a high wind and rain that fell like steel rods. We had better turn back. But C.S.R. would not do so, wherefore we drove on. It was impossible to read any road signs, and at that speed it would have been even in a blaze of sunshine! I remember approaching Dijon towards dawn, when we were about two hours behind the record.

But the car never faltered; nor did the British-made tyres let us down . . .

Of course, with the coming of the sunlight and the passing of the stormy and chilly night, we were all as blithe as birds. Thereafter everything went even better than our most sanguine expectations. To see that little car recover those lost two hours and begin beating the record a second time as a day advanced was a heartening revelation. We reached Boulogne – 771 miles from the start, traversed in 28 hours 14 minutes, including all stops, loss of direction and the night storm – and had 3 hours 11 minutes to wait on Boulogne Quay before preparations for departure commenced.

In spite of that long wait and all the other hazards the record was beaten by just one and a half minutes.

By this time Rolls-Royces had been well blooded in competition. Claude Johnson was quick to understand that building a superb motor car was one thing, and selling it quite another. All his activity in the next few years was therefore devoted towards exploiting every means available to din into the public consciousness the supreme excellence of Royce's cars. So successful was he that by 1914 he had built up the Rolls-Royce legend into a reputation that towered over all rivals. Not until February 1971 did that tower begin to totter.

In the early days of motoring there were none of the scientifically conducted tests that motoring magazines perform on new models today. Really Johnson had only one way of making his point – to set a standard of achievement that others could not match and to publicise that achievement as loudly as possible. The most obvious and effective method of accomplishing both these ends was to compete in races – and to win. Such a policy entirely depended on Royce's cars being as supreme in reality as they were in the legend. An early opportunity of demonstrating this occurred in the 1905 Isle of Man Tourist Trophy, and Rolls immediately entered two Twenties.

The Isle of Man remains a racing centre to this day. It owes this position to the fact that at the beginning of the century the government, horrified by the continental example, would not tolerate the sport in England. Early racing on the continent had proved exceedingly dangerous to participants and spectators alike, for in the search for speed more and more powerful engines had been crammed into the most flimsy chassis. The cars that resulted were giants with bones of clay; and while their achievements were remarkable (in 1902 a car averaged 70 m.p.h. on the first 50 miles of the Paris–Vienna race), so was the number of fatalities they caused. The culmination of horror was reached in the 1903 Paris–Madrid race, which the English papers called 'The Race to Death' because of the number killed. But English enthusiasts were undeterred, and in the legislative independence of the Manxmen they found a way of circumventing their government's ban. Fortunately for Rolls-Royce, the English racing authorities determined on a form of racing that would test qualities other than sheer speed. Only a limited amount of petrol was to be allowed for each race, and all cars, which must be of standard type, had to compete with one passenger and ballast equivalent to two others in the back. These were conditions ideally designed for Royce's talent; huge engines being out of the question owing to the petrol limitation, it was essentially the cars' efficiency which was under test.

As ever, Rolls left nothing to chance. He took a car to the Isle of Man to spy out the land and gauge the best gear ratios; he made trial runs to test petrol consumption and decide on the right-sized engine to use. In the event Rolls-Royce entered two Twenties. In order not to run the risk of both having empty tanks before the end of the race, one had a slightly smaller engine. To save petrol and increase speed Royce introduced an overdrive gear, called 'sprinting gear' as opposed to 'direct drive' (normal top gear). A month before the race no motoring expert would have given the Rolls-Royces any chance: everyone knew of their reliability and quietness but few imagined that they had the speed necessary to carry them to victory. Then Rolls averaged 33 m.p.h. on a practice run and the cognoscenti began to think again. Not for long though: on the first of the four 52-mile laps Rolls's gearbox packed up. The air was heavy with suspicions of sabotage and parts of the gearbox were examined in the search for evidence. *Autocar* found the event so serious – a Rolls-Royce defaulting for no apparent reason – that they recorded it in capital letters for heavy emphasis. 'There was A CRACK, AND THE GEARS HAD PARTED . . .' The topic was as highly charged as the vexed question of whether some bounders had fitted false bottoms to petrol tanks. Rolls was furious but was probably himself to blame for having attempted to get into gear when the car was coasting too fast down hill.

Now all Rolls-Royce hopes centred on Northey, driving the smaller car. His speeds mounted until on the third lap he recorded the fastest time, 34·1 m.p.h. His was the first car to finish but an Arrol-Johnson which had started later just snatched the victory, with an average speed of 33·9 m.p.h. compared with Northey's 33·7 m.p.h. But Northey had made the fastest non-stop run, and

Rolls-Royce's reputation soared. When one considers the massive dignity which now characterises their image it is odd to remember that they first exploded into the limelight for sporting achievement. Soon after the *Autocar* wrote a glowing review of the Twenty '. . . we are fain to characterise this vehicle as an ideal light touring car, running with extraordinary smoothness and silkiness, and climbing hills on the direct third and geared fourth in the most remarkable manner.'

But Rolls was not content with second place for his car and immediately entered for the 1906 Tourist Trophy. This time, the fortunes of the two Rolls-Royce drivers were reversed, Northey having to retire due to a broken spring on lap one, and Rolls cruising home to win easily. Northey dispatched a sad telegram to Royce in Manchester – 'Broken spring, broken heart' to which Royce returned 'Imagine our regret when we consider that we have robbed you of a place at least by giving you that confounded spring.' But Rolls-Royce did all right for Northey, who later joined the company with the duties of making technical criticisms of new models. He quickly decided that since so many Rolls-Royce owners travelled extensively on the continent this task could most effectively be discharged from a base in Paris. On one occasion the company received enthusiastic reports from him about a new steering system he had been asked to test, only to discover that by an oversight it had not in fact been installed in Northey's car. 'I hear that the steering's done the dirty on us,' was his reaction.

Rolls's response to the congratulations he received on his victory was typically generous – 'as I had nothing to do but to sit there and wait until the car got to the finish the credit is obviously to Mr. Royce, the designer and builder.' Mr. Royce at this time was designing and building his masterpiece.

The Silver Ghost is the most famous car ever made. It first appeared at the very end of 1906 and reigned superbly over the motoring scene until until 1925, a link between the beginnings and the Middle Ages of motoring. This was by far the longest selling production model of those times, and altogether over 6,000 Silver Ghosts were produced. The new car's chassis was derived from the early 30 h.p. model, which had been perhaps the least perfect of Royce's early output, and the gulf separating the two cars demonstrates the marvellous effects of Royce's patient dedication to the improvement of all he touched. For the Ghost Royce had designed a new six-cylinder 48 h.p. side-valve engine which few modern cars have improved on for quietness. Further, so free from vibration was the chassis that it was possible to balance a penny on its edge on the top of the bonnet while the engine was running. Another Silver Ghost party trick was to place a glass brimful of water on the bonnet: not a drop was spilt even when the engine was raced up to 1,600 revolutions per minute. Perhaps most remarkable of all the car's characteristics was the flexibility of the engine and transmission system; one could accelerate effortlessly from 3 to 60 m.p.h. in top gear without a trace of hesitation or spluttering. This was an alluring sales point at a time when many drivers, often with justice, regarded changing gear with extreme alarm; the custom was to start in first gear and change into top immediately. Realistically the Silver Ghost manual recognised the inexperience of early motorists by providing the following instruction: 'Should there be any doubts about ascending a steep hill, the car should be dropped on to the lowest gear at the *bottom of the hill* rather than the gear changed on the hill.' But there were few hills which the Silver Ghost could not effortlessly crest in top; indeed, in tests it was driven from London to Edinburgh using just top gear.

For the technically inclined here is a contemporary account of the engine:

The six-cylinder Rolls-Royce is unique in three particulars:

1. Mr. Royce is of the opinion that a six-cylinder engine should be treated as two engines of three cylinders each rather than considering them, as is usually done, as three engines of two cylinders each. He maintains that the 'couple' occurs between the two sets of three cylinders and at the two ends of the crank-shaft, and it is at these three points that specially large bearings should be provided. The Rolls-Royce crank-shaft, in addition to these three bearings, has four intermediate bearings.

2. Mr. Royce is of the opinion that under certain road conditions the forward end of the frame might have a tendency to 'whip', or bend slightly out of line, and that if the six-cylinder engine with its long crank-case were fixed rigidly to the frame, considerable strain might be put on the crank-case. He has ingeniously met this possibility by providing a three-point suspension, so that the forward end of the engine is quite unaffected by the position of the side members of the frame.

3. The last point is that the radiator for a similar reason is insulated. It can move backwards, forwards or sideways, and is not rigidly attached to any part of the chassis, and therefore is not subject to the shocks which often cause leakage and breakage.

The engine is fitted with two complete systems of ignition, high-tension magneto and high-tension accumulator . . .

A cone clutch lined with leather is employed, which practically runs in oil, and is therefore very sweet in its action. The gearbox has four forward speeds and one reverse, the third speed being the direct drive. The fourth gear is used for really fast road work.

The makers of this car pride themselves on its ease of suspension. The springs are made of a large number of thin plates, instead of following the usual practice of a small number of thick plates . . .

The chassis price of this car is £895.

Such a car was like manna from heaven for a publicist of Claude Johnson's gifts. Even before he set to work the *Autocar* had provided a rave review:

The running of this car at slow speeds is the smoothest thing we have experienced while for silence the engine beneath the bonnet

might be a sewing machine . . . At whatever speed this car is being
driven on its direct third, there is *no* engine so far as sensation goes,
nor are one's auditory nerves troubled driving or standing by a
fuller sound than enamates from an eight day clock. There is no
realisation of driving propulsion; the feeling as the passenger sits
either at the front or the back of the vehicle is one of being wafted
through the landscape.

The *Autocar*'s 'auditory nerves' must soon have been troubled
by Johnson's advertising campaign. He knew he could rely
absolutely on the car in any test so he invited the R.A.C. to
observe its achievements.

First the Ghost demonstrated its hill-climbing prowess. It
carried four passengers up Netherhall Gardens in Hampstead
(gradient 1 in 7) in second gear and then did 42 m.p.h. on the flat
in the same gear. Still burdened with the patient four the Ghost
successfully tackled the test hill in Richmond Park (gradient 1 in
7) using third only and in this gear it clocked up 53 m.p.h. But
these achievements were only preliminaries to an attempt on the
world record for a non-stop reliability run, at that time held by a
Siddeley with 7,089 miles. This attempt comprehended participa-
tion in the Scottish reliability trial where the Ghost won the gold
medal. Thereafter a team of drivers (including Rolls) drove it day
and night up and down between London and Glasgow until
15,000 miles were completed. The engine was always kept running except on Sundays when the car was locked in a garage. At
the 629th mile, during the Scottish trial, there had been a one
minute stoppage due to a petrol tap being shaken shut, but the
remaining 14,371 miles were completely trouble free. Johnson had
not finished yet: he now asked the R.A.C. supervisors to strip
down the engine, inspect the parts for wear, and give instructions
regarding what needed renewing to make the car 'as good as
new'. The engine was passed as perfect; one or two parts of the
steering showed very slight wear, about one thousandth of an
inch, which the committee considered not as good as new. The
small universal joints in the magneto drive likewise failed to pass
their scrutiny; and the water pump needed repacking. That was
all. The total bill for these replacements was £2 2s. 7d. Unfortunately all early tyres were apt to give trouble and several new
ones had been required on the ceaseless journey. Even including
this expense, however, the cost of running the car came to just
4½d. per mile.

By the standards of the day this was unheard-of reliability and
naturally 'C.J.' broadcast it from the rooftops. He himself was
responsible for the name 'Silver Ghost', taking the thirteenth
model and adorning the coachwork with silver. Did he remember
the *Country Life* description of Royce's 10 h.p. as 'ghost-like'
when he coined the phrase? One of the original Silver Ghosts can
be seen at the Rolls-Royce showrooms in Conduit Street. Despite
its venerable age and the half million miles it has covered this

car could still win any reliability trial. Indeed, it recently proved
it with a top-gear only, faultless run to Scotland, to commemor-
ate the former triumphs. And when in 1969 this Silver Ghost
traversed America the only trouble during the entire trip came,
as in 1907, from the tyres. Incidentally the Silver Ghost, quite
apart from providing years of trouble free motoring, has been an
excellent investment. A 1912 model was recently sold in London
for £10,000. Not bad considering the depreciation rates on
modern cars!

VIII

Before the Silver Ghost appeared Rolls-Royce had ceased to be
just a name and become a company. Encouraged by the quick
success of their association Rolls and Royce took the plunge and
merged into a more formal partnership. On 16 March 1906, after
a gestation period of fifteen months there was born the company
of Rolls-Royce Ltd., with a capital of £60,000, £10,000 of which
was contributed by Rolls. C. S. Rolls & Co. disappeared altogether in the merger, thus ending Rolls's sales of other makes
of cars. (Interestingly, Royce's cars had not been Rolls's only
entries to the Isle of Man T.T.). The electrical side of the Cook
Street business continued to operate under the name of Royce
alone until after his death but he ceded the motor car side to the
new company. The first directors were Royce, Rolls, Johnson
and a Yorkshireman called Briggs who had encouraged the
merger.

Almost immediately Rolls-Royce Ltd. made two important
decisions. The first, made in 1906, was that it was impossible to
continue production in the restricted conditions at Cook Street.
A careful study was made to find the most suitable place for
Rolls-Royce's needs and the choice was narrowed down to
Leicester or Derby. When Derby offered electrical power at
especially cheap rates the matter was settled and a site of 12⅔
acres soon purchased. Although he was heavily engaged on the
Silver Ghost's development, Royce somehow found time to
design most of the factory buildings himself, and very well too.
The new factory was officially opened in July 1908.

The move, however, had necessitated a considerable increase
in the capital of the company, to £200,000. £100,000 worth of
shares were issued to the public on 6 December 1906, with the
stipulation that unless £50,000 was provided within a certain
time the flotation would be abandoned. With the time limit
almost reached, only £41,000 had been subscribed and the whole
move appeared in jeopardy. The situation was saved by Briggs,
Rolls-Royce's first devoted admirer, who provided £10,000 in
the nick of time. When Briggs died in 1919, de Looze, the company secretary, insisted on the annual report being edged with

black, in gratitude for this last-minute reprieve. For Briggs himself there were more earthly compensations. The company prospered and the share price with it. Anybody who had invested £1,000 in 1906 would have acquired £1,500 shares free, by way of bonus issues, in the next forty-three years, at the end of which time his total of 2,500 shares could have been sold for nearly £12,000, a profit of £11,000. In addition he would have received £10,000 in dividends. More recent shareholders may be forgiven for regarding these figures with a certain amount of disgust.

The company's prospectus offering these first shares to the public also disclosed the salaries of the leading figures. Royce as chief engineer and works director received £1,250 p.a. and 4 per cent of the profits in excess of £10,000; Rolls as technical managing director £750 per annum and 4 per cent of the surplus profits, and Claremont, Royce's original partner, was chairman and commercial adviser at £250 p.a. and 2 per cent of the surplus profits. Poor Claremont, the days were far off when he had been the capitalist behind Royce's first company.

The other vital decision made by the young company concerned the Silver Ghost. Claude Johnson had always seen the potential in the six-cylinder market and now that Royce had produced a model that outstripped all competitors he determined to exploit that potential for all it was worth. At a board-meeting on 8 March 1908 he carried a policy that in future Rolls-Royce should concentrate exclusively on this one model. It is reported that Royce himself was not enthused by this decision but there is little doubt of its correctness. Instead of exercising his minute attention to detail and his passion for improvement on four cars Royce could now concentrate his talent on bringing one car to a pitch of perfection.

To many it might have appeared that this had already been attained. The years before the First War saw the Silver Ghost piling triumph on triumph. In the autumn of 1907 it made its debut in America, at the New York Motor Show where it won much applause. Rolls-Royce's first brush with the New World had not been so happy; in December 1906 Rolls took one of the T.T. Twenties to compete in New York. He duly won in his class but was rash enough, and brave enough, to make some disparaging remarks about the quality of American cars which he considered badly made. Inevitably, a considerable rumpus ensued and Rolls was challenged to a race to Chicago and back. Disdainfully leaving the glove on the ground Rolls returned a lofty answer to the effect that he would welcome the challenger's entry into the Isle of Man T.T. in which other qualities besides mere speed, such as reliability and petrol consumption, were also assessed. Despite this imbroglio Rolls found time on that first visit to appoint an American representative and the United States has always been a good customer for Rolls-Royce's cars.

In England a Silver Ghost won the 1908 International Touring
Club Trial, especially distinguishing itself in the hill climbing
events. Johnson, ever seeking publicity for the car, offered a
challenge of £1,000 to any car in the same class to follow the
trial with a 15,000-mile reliability run, but nobody accepted.
They may have felt that 1/4d (7p) a mile was an inadequate
return for 15,000 miles driving. In 1919 there was a final show-
down with Napiers. Selwyn Edge, who was as determined a
publicist for Napiers as Johnson was for Rolls-Royce, realised
that his cars must give way to the Rolls-Royce as far as reliability
and silence were concerned, yet hoped to prove convincingly that
in performance his car was in the lead. A hotted-up, but basically
standard Napier was driven in top gear only from London to
Edinburgh under R.A.C. surveillance, recording a fuel consumption of 19·35 m.p.g.; and then taken to Brooklands where it was
timed at 76·42 m.p.h. 'C.J.' was unable to resist the challenge
and a slightly smaller Rolls-Royce improved on these figures
with 24·32 m.p.g. and a top speed of 78·26 m.p.h. Incidentally,
this car was driven by E. W. Hives, later to become Managing
Director of Rolls-Royce. From that moment Rolls-Royce stood
alone, unchallenged in reputation by any contemporary make.
Henceforward the car's achievements only confirmed expectations; there was little to add to its lustre. In 1911, nevertheless,
Rolls-Royce won the Empress of Germany's Cup in the Prince
Henry tour; and a specially streamlined version of the London to
Edinburgh model achieved 101 m.p.h. over a quarter of a mile at
Brooklands.

The suddenly there was an abrupt and rude check to the
car's triumphs. In the 1912 Austrian Alpine trial a Rolls-Royce,
carrying four passengers, and driven by James Radley, proved
unable to climb one of the hills. The Silver Ghost's reputation
tottered; nothing seems more fallible than infallibility dis-
proved. In fact there was a perfectly good reason for this mishap.
In order to prevent drivers using overdrive top, which was not
entirely silent, Royce had cut it out and substituted a three-
speed gear box. While the bottom gear was quite low enough to
enable the Silver Ghost to tackle any English hill, it did not cater
for the exceptional steepness of the Austrian passes. But Rolls-
Royce would not content themselves with just substituting
different gear ratios; typically the company sent out a team of
engineers to the Alps where they measured the steepness of every
incline and the angle of every bend in the trial course. A factor
also taken into account was the thinness of atmosphere at those
heights, which made cooling more of a problem. The results of
these investigations were brought back to Royce who produced
a specially modified version of the Silver Ghost, henceforward
known as the Continental. The stain of the 1912 catastrophe had
to be blotted out by the triumphs of this model in 1913.

The company entered three cars for the 1913 Alpine trial and

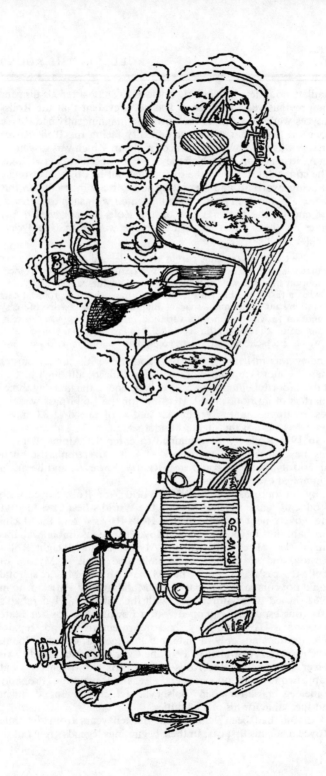

Radley, doubtless particularly anxious to shine after his disaster the previous year, another. It was soon evident that the Rolls-Royces were in a class of their own. So magnificently had Royce done his work that the worst difficulty facing the Rolls-Royce drivers was the slowness of the official car, which was driven by an Austrian count and which they were supposed not to overtake. The count did not mind the overtaking but he objected strongly to being sworn at, and there were some tricky moments on this score. The nineteen passes were navigated with such ease that at the end of the trial not one of the Rolls-Royces needed any water in their radiators. The *Autocar* was moved to lyrical flights:

> The Rolls-Royces came past in great style, and I am bound to say that I have never seen anything more beautiful in the way of loco-motion than the way in which they flew up the pass. We all know what a fast car is like on the level, but the sight of a group of cars running up a mountain road at high speed, with a superbly easy motion to which each little variation in the surface gave the sem-blance of a greyhound in its stride, was inspiring to a degree . . . it was a spectacle, indeed, worth going many a long mile to see.

Radley was in irrepressible form and drove his car far harder than the more cautious works drivers. Indeed, although he had started fourth behind the works cars he ended the first day three-quarters of an hour ahead. His time for the Loibl pass was the best by three minutes, yet his car had a top speed of 82 m.p.h. and was thus not the slightest undergeared.

In 1914 Rolls-Royce disdained to enter the Alpine Trial; it has never been the company's style to overemphasise their superiority. Nothing could stop Radley, however, and he again triumphed overwhelmingly.

By the outbreak of the First World War Rolls-Royce were producing what was indisputably the World's Best Car. In 1911 the government ordered eight Rolls-Royces for the Delhi Durbah, thus introducing Rolls-Royce to the insatiable Mahara-jah market. The Maharajah of Mysore acquired eight Rolls-Royces, and so created a new collective noun, a 'Mysore of Rolls-Royces'. But even the Maharajah of Mysore's total could not compare with that of the Maharajah of Patiala who in 1962 owned twenty-three, nor with the Nizam of Hyderabad's fifty (one especially equipped with a howdah-like top for State occasions). The company had representatives and repairs organisations not only in India but in America, Canada, Spain, Austria, even Australia. In 1914 the Czar of Russia bought two Silver Ghosts from the Rolls-Royce Paris showrooms – what happened to them, one wonders, after the Revolution. Probably some egalitarian-minded Bolshevik reluctantly found them indispensable for his official duties.

All this had been achieved in just ten years from the time Royce made his first car. In their beginnings legends grow out of fact; Royce had provided these facts and Johnson had made them generally known. Put like that it sounds simple, but, as we shall see, the intense labour of those years came close to destroying the great mechanic.

The other partner, Rolls, had tended to drift away from motoring since 1907 when he met Wilbur Wright who took him up in his remarkable heavier-than-air flying machine. The event immediately hooked Rolls on to a new craze and inspired him to one of his most Toad-like effusions:

> . . . after experimenting with every form of locomotion including cycle and motor racing, a voyage in the dirigible of the French army and over 130 trips in an ordinary bàlloon, there is nothing so fascinating and exhilarating as flying. It gives one an entirely new sense of life. The power of flight is as a fresh gift from the Creator, the greatest treasure yet given to man and one, I believe, destined to work great changes in human life as I know it today.

Destined too, one might add, to destroy the company which gave him a toehold on the immortality he had desired. But Rolls should not be mocked; his enthusiasm was sincere and his prophecies have been fulfilled. Moreover, his contributions to flying were as important as those he made to motoring. The War Office engaged him to train pilots. He was one of the originators of the Royal Aero Club and was a seminal influence in the founding of Shorts Brothers, the aircraft manufacturers. Inevitably, however, his interest in and association with Rolls-Royce declined. This was the more the case since, try as he would, he could not persuade Royce to design an aircraft engine. In April 1910 Rolls resigned as managing director of the company. Three months later, on 11 July 1910, his plane crashed during a competition at Bournemouth, and he was instantly killed. There is a poignant photograph, which makes as good an epitaph as any for Rolls, of this ill-fated plane being towed away by a Silver Ghost.

Into Top Gear

I

Modern war has been good for technological development; the bigger the war, the more startling the advances that are made. The search for more horribly effective weapons of destruction, especially when stimulated by fear of the enemy, marvellously concentrates the energies and inventiveness of man. It follows that the catastrophe of the 1914–18 war, in which some nine millions were killed, saw correspondingly huge technological advances. To give but one example: when, in 1913, the *Daily Mail* offered £10,000 to the first men to fly the Atlantic there was considerable mirth at the impossibility of the challenge, but after the war the prize was claimed within a year. In this particular development, as in so many others, Rolls-Royce, as we shall see, played a considerable part.

Although the heads of the British army had grasped (wrongly) that the next war would be a war of movement, they had failed to comprehend that the movement might be mechanical. In August 1914 the British army had a total stock of precisely eighty motor vehicles; and although by 1918 this number had increased to over 100,000, some 700,000 horses were kept in France throughout the war. A tractor which had been demonstrated to the army before the war was contemptuously dismissed: 'Its noise and smell in a column are intolerable and very few horses will pass it.' The reasoning was revealing. The army did, though, have confidence in *steam* tractors. Arguably the first self-propelled vehicle to be produced was Cugnot's steam tractor of 1769; it had been rejected by the army of the 'ancien regime'. In 1914, however, the British army manifested more faith in the military applications of this form of vehicle and dispatched a number to France, whence they never returned. The angels at Mons had quite enough on their hands fighting for their particular care, the British soldier, without bothering themselves with rescuing his steam tractors.

In this chronic state of unreadiness for modern warfare Eng-

38

land at least had a priceless asset in the possession of the world's most reliable car. Sir John French, the Commander-in-Chief, was immediately provided with a Rolls-Royce in which, as those who have seen the film 'Oh, what a Lovely War' will recall, he undertook tours of inspection and reconnaissance along our lines. A group of twenty-five keen drivers voluntarily associated to form the Royal Automobile Club Corps. Inevitably some of them were Rolls-Royce owners, including the Duke of Westminster and the hero of the 1913 and 1914 Alpine trials, James Radley. In the early weeks of the war in France they did invaluable work ferrying top officers to important conferences. At this time there was no well-defined 'front' between the armies and on several occasions the Rolls-Royces clashed with roving bands of Uhlans (German cavalry). The Duke of Westminster proved especially formidable in this context; he kept a rifle handy in his Rolls and used to take pot-shots at the Uhlans as the car raced along. In such manner do the recreations of the English aristocracy come to the nation's aid in time of war. Until December 1916 a team of four Rolls-Royces was responsible for the King's messenger services between the British G.H.Q. and the French ports. In the two years of their service not one of these cars ever broke down.

The course of the war very quickly showed what an error the neglect of mechanisation had been. As the German armies swept through Belgium, a group of Belgian officers who possessed a few ordinary touring cars with improvised side-armour of boiler plate, and mounting a machine gun, managed to harass them most effectively. In 1899 F. R. Sims (crouching behind the armour but complete with bowler hat) had demonstrated his motor quadricycle with a Maxim machine gun mounted on the handlebars, but his ideas had been laughingly dismissed. Undeterred, in 1902 Simms had produced his 'war car', an open-topped armoured vehicle carrying two machine guns on pedestal mountings. The war car weighed $5\frac{1}{2}$ tons and despite a 15 h.p. engine and four gears, could achieve a top speed of only 9 m.p.h. This vehicle appeared at the Crystal Palace where a photograph shows it surrounded by a number of admirers. But there is no doubt that Simms' ideas were ahead of their time so, naturally, the army took no interest.

In 1914, therefore, when the usefulness of armoured cars had been demonstrated by the Belgians, the military had no choice but to follow their example and cloak ordinary touring cars with armour. (Actually, by some typically British quirk, this task was initially entrusted to the Navy.) Many makes of car were used for this purpose, but naturally the Rolls-Royce, owing to its demonstrated reliability, was the most effective model. By March 1915 there were seventy-eight Rolls-Royce armoured cars, compared with thirty-six Lanchesters and thirty Seabrooks. So the car which Royce's talents had created to satisfy the perfectionist whims of a tiny elite of pioneer motorists became overnight an

important defence weapon. The company stopped deliveries for private customers immediately the war broke out.

At first, the Admiralty produced a temporary design, with no turret but with a protected crew and engine and a mounted machine gun. Soon, though, a more permanent type emerged, which, for the Silver Ghost chassis, provided a test such as Royce himself might have invented in one of his more sadistic moments. Plating three-eighths of an inch thick increased the weight of the car by three tons, but the only alteration found necessary to the chassis was the fitting of thirteen leaf springs in front and fifteen at the rear. Later the back wheels were doubled up. The engine remained unchanged but under favourable conditions could still take the car up to 70 m.p.h. Moreover, somehow or other the Rolls managed to retain much of its civilian elegance. A Maxim machine gun was installed in a turret five feet across, behind which was an open platform. Armour plating also covered the car's bonnet, and in front of the radiator a pair of doors could be opened or closed according to whether protection was required. Naturally when they were closed the radiator tended to overheat, one of the few problems caused by the conversion. Safety demanded that the driver's vision be restricted to just a tiny slit.

The first squadron of Rolls-Royce cars was equipped by the end of 1914 and was sent for training to the East Coast where it was feared a German invasion was imminent. The cars proved completely reliable and by January 1915 there were eight squadrons complete, except for machine guns, which the Navy was eventually able to commandeer. By that time, however, the armies were dug in from the sea to Switzerland, and the car's usefulness in France had become extremely limited. All the same a squadron was sent under the intrepid Duke of Westminster and saw a little action, the most impressive being the capture of the village of Roisel. Two Rolls-Royces simply drove into the middle of the village and took control before the Germans could summon sufficient fire power to pierce their armour. For the remainder of the war, though, the role of the armoured cars was necessarily restricted to the side shows in Africa and the Middle East. Two Rolls-Royce squadrons accompanied the army on the ill-fated Gallipoli venture, but the cars spent most of their time stationary in the protection of a deep trench. They were soon evacuated to Egypt where the flatter country was far more suitable for their operations.

When a Rolls-Royce squadron (again led by the Duke of Westminster) landed at Walfisch Bay in German South West Africa in 1915, the going was at first so rough that the cars had to be sent fifty miles inland by rail. Even here conditions were such as to destroy any normal vehicle; there was no semblance of a road and the landscape was all scrub and rocks, making the pre-war reliability tests the Silver Ghost had undergone look like Sunday afternoon dawdles. But the armoured cars took it all in their stride and played an important part in the success of the South West African campaign. They were used to ambush the enemy, and at night their headlights served to show up targets. Rolls-Royces were also in service in East Africa, where their performance was such that the natives apparently credited them with supernatural powers. Henry Royce would doubtless have explained to them that there was no magic save extremely hard work.

The Duke of Westminster's squadron had meanwhile been transferred to Egypt where the cars were used to defend the Suez canal, and in the Western desert against hostile tribes, in particular the Senussi. When the S.S. *Tara* was sunk by a German submarine in the Mediterranean and the survivors fell into Senussi hands, a force of armoured cars, including nine Rolls-Royces, made a hundred-mile dash across the desert to rescue them. In spite of only primitive skills in desert navigation and constant trouble with tyres, all the cars reached Bir-Hakim where the prisoners were held; and the Senussi, unable to match the cars' mobility and fire power, were easily overcome. The *Tara*'s survivors were duly rescued but the episode was marred by a disgraceful massacre of the Senussi, who were machine gunned to a man.

In Mesopotamia there was a thrilling chase when a Rolls-Royce armoured car pursued a Mercedes at over 60 m.p.h. across the desert. The encounter ended as all such encounters (at least those reported) did in the days when British was best: the Mercedes was slowly overhauled and a few bursts of machine gun fire put it out of action. It was in the Middle East too that the armoured cars' most renowned exploits – those associated with T. E. Lawrence – took place.

Lawrence appreciated that 'all the Turks in Arabia could not fight a single Rolls-Royce'. Fortunately, to make assurance doubly sure, he managed to requisition nine, and used them extensively both for reconnaissance and for his speciality, railway destruction. On one occasion Lawrence blew up two bridges, destroyed 600 pairs of rails, captured two Turkish posts and smashed a Turkish cavalry regiment in a single day, with only three Rolls-Royces. On another raid a spring bracket on one of the cars gave way, but fortunately the driver (appositely named Rolls) managed to effect temporary repairs by wedging the spring into position with pieces of wood attached to the running board.

'A Rolls in the desert was above rubies' Lawrence reported, 'and though we had been driving in them for eighteen months, not upon the polished roads of their maker's invention, but across country of the vilest, at speed, day or night, carrying a ton of goods, and four or five men up, yet this was our first structural accident in the team of nine . . . In camp we stitched the blocks with captured telephone wire and bound them together and to the chassis and the spring to the chassis, till it looked as strong as possible and we put back the load. So enduring was the running board that we did the ordinary work with the car for the next six weeks, and took her into Damascus at the end. Great was Rolls, and great was Royce! They were worth hundreds of men to us in these deserts.'

Lawrence called such campaigning 'fighting de-luxe', but had several narrow escapes, especially once when pursued by a Turkish plane dropping bombs.

'We crept on defencelessly, slowly, among the stones,' he recalled, 'feeling more and more like sardines in a doomed tin, as the bombs fell closer. One sent a shower of small stuff through the driving slit of the car, but only cut our knuckles. One tore off the front tyre, and nearly lurched the car over.'

The Rolls-Royce engine, though, continued to purr away and returned Lawrence and his companions to safety.

After the war, on being asked if there was anything to be bought that he couldn't afford, but would like to have, Lawrence replied 'I should like to have a Rolls-Royce car with enough tyres and petrol to last me all my life.' To his fawning anecdotalist this was evidence of his simplicity and humanity, though these are not qualities which, however unfairly, one instinctively associates with Rolls-Royce owners. In view of Lawrence's death on a motor cycle, however, it seems a pity that his 'simple' and 'human' request was not granted. At least he would have found it hard as a Rolls-Royce owner to plunge into ostentatious anonymity as a private in the Air Force. It proved difficult enough without one.

In his role of Aircraftsman Shaw, Lawrence met Royce after the war at Calshot air base where the Schneider Trophy engines were being tuned up. Royce was amazed – 'Who would have thought that little fellow would be Lawrence of Arabia? I can hardly believe it.' A witness reports that

'it never occurred to him [Royce] that he was probably a much greater man than the Lawrence who caused a stir every time he walked across the air base.'

Altogether, the performance of the armoured cars in the First War much enhanced the Rolls-Royce legend. There were few breakdowns; even the appalling physical conditions encountered could not match the severity of Royce's standards. The dreaded Russian winter failed to worst one Rolls-Royce (an ordinary, non-armoured version) which a British officer, Commander Locker-Lampson, drove 53,000 miles over the Caucasian mountains, and beyond, at temperatures sometimes 40° below zero. At the journey's end only the front springs and a ball-race in one of the front wheels needed replacing. Small wonder that the war-time drivers became such fervent admirers of Rolls-Royce. Some of the armoured cars survived to see service in the Second World War. A fitting epitaph to their durability was the example of one Rolls-Royce armoured car which served in India and

Afghanistan from 1915 to 1940. It was nick-named 'Wedding
Bells' because in 1920 it was pressed into service as a bridal carriage. Even when demolished it did not wholly die, as a com-
memorative cigarette lighter was made from part of the engine.

II

In recent years over eighty per cent of Rolls-Royce's business has
been the manufacture of aeroplane engines so that it is surprising
to discover that Royce was initially curiously reluctant, despite
the persuasions of Rolls and 'C.J.', to concern himself with their
design. (Indeed, even when he had won great renown in this field
something of the same reluctance persisted, in that he never in his
life went up in an aeroplane). In 1914, however, the Government
ordered Rolls-Royce to produce some aero-engines of French
design, and one which so disgusted Royce that he immediately
set about producing his own plans to rescue his factory from the
unworthy and alien engines.

In one sense, however, it was his factory no longer. Indeed he
had hardly set foot in it for four years. In 1910 his health had
completely collapsed. The years of endless concentrated labour
and malnutrition suddenly claimed their toll in the form of severe
intestinal disorders and doctors despaired of his life. That he survived was due to Claude Johnson who was both devoted to
Royce and understood just how much the company depended on
his talent. Johnson took him on a long tour abroad, ranging as
far as Egypt. Returning by way of the Riviera, they happened on
what was then the remote and wild village (just two villas and a
hotel) of Le Canadel. Looking out at the view, Royce murmured
'I should like to live here.' The attentive 'C.J.' caught the sound
and, ever the organisation man, discreetly slipped away to render
the vaguely-formed desire a fact. By that evening he was able to
inform Royce that building could begin whenever he wished.
Here indeed, far more than in travel, was the tonic which Royce
needed. The use of leisure is an art no less than application to
work is a virtue, and it was an art that Royce had had no opportunity to acquire. Now, though, he plunged into the design of the
house, becoming absorbed as was his wont with every detail,
down to the fitting of the window frames and the hinges of the
doors. All his obsessive perfectionism was turned on to architec-
ture. The builder was rash enough to try to save slates by making
the roof a few degrees flatter, but the eye of the master noted it
and the builder must needs begin the roof again. When the house
was re-opened after the First War it was found that no dust at all
had got in, so accurately had Royce done his work.

Thereafter, in peacetime at least, he habitually wintered at Le
Canadel and spent his summers in England, first at Crow-
borough in Sussex, and later at West Wittering, near Chichester.

He hardly ever visited Derby again. Because the doctors recommended that Royce should live by the sea 'C.J.' set up a team of designers to work with him both in the country and at Le Canadel. They were housed in a separate annexe in conditions of considerable austerity; Royce forbade even a telephone lest it should prove a distraction. The system worked well. Churchill once remarked that a committee trying to produce a horse is apt to end up by producing a camel, but Royce never allowed this kind of thing to happen, always remaining in control, while yet involving his team in every decision. Much credit is also due to A. G. Elliott who was his chief assistant for many years.

Such were the conditions under which Royce built his first aero-engine. The facility with which he was able to adapt his talent to such a mammoth and complex task is remarkable when his complete lack of any mathematical education is remembered. He never even used a slide-rule, seeming to know by instinct what others discovered by calculation. He approached the new problem in the same way that he tackled all engineering posers – through practical experiment. 'Providing one has sufficient patience there is no such thing as an insoluble problem' was always his motto. Every day a battery of instructions was sent to Derby and later 'C.J.' had these letters printed in a severely limited edition and distributed (marked 'strictly private and confidential') amongst senior Rolls-Royce officials. This collection became known as the 'Rolls-Royce Bible', a condensed gospel of engineering principles according to Royce. Secrecy having been relaxed a little since Johnson's day we are at liberty to quote some extracts:

Re Aero Engine Cylinders
With reference to the aero cylinder tools, any way that the first sample cylinders can be produced with temporary tools will please me. It is necessary, however, if we make tools that are at all costly, that they should be made thoroughly well, so as to be lasting and achieve their object without any nursing. This cylinder work is so important that nothing is too good to produce it so that the parts of the engine will go together without hesitation, and be interchangeable.

I am quite willing for you to alter any designs that I send, providing that they will carry out their duties satisfactorily, but I do not think it worth while to alter them seriously because they may, in the form I send them, be thought rather expensive.

Re R.A.F. Aero Engines
Referring to the high-class finish, we are not people that put a high finish on parts unless it is necessary, and I quite agree that on this work no money should be spent on unnecessary finish, but spend all the money and time necessary to make a good and reliable working job of the highest possible efficiency.

Re 200 h.p. Aero-Engine
We do not believe that it is possible to test them to destruction, but we should very much like to do so, if any satisfactory means can be found of repeating the load thousands of times. This we may do later.

Re Aluminium Pistons

This subject will bear investigation, and for your part I recommend that one of the pistons only on an engine be made larger than the other eleven, in fact, so large in the top that you know when the throttle is suddenly opened it will probably pull up the engine with its tightness. We can then let this piston be fitted to an articulated rod, and can pull up the engine a few times with this piston, providing that nothing breaks on the first occasion. Should the piston or connecting rod give way, the experiments will be fairly conclusive and very instructive.

Always the same insistence on high standards, the same determination to test every part to its uttermost. The engine which finally emerged after only six months from these ruthlessly demanding techniques was the 200 h.p. Eagle, at least it *began* by being 200 h.p. Like all good aero-engines it had 'stretch' potential, that is to say the designer was able continuously to modify the basic design to produce ever-greater power. Thus what began as a 200 h.p. engine had grown to 360 h.p. by the end of the war.

As Royce had used the same methods so the Eagle engine had the same virtues as his motor cars. It powered not only the F.E.2d fighter, but also the Handley-Page 0.400 twin-engined bomber, the Fairey IIIb seaplane and the Vickers Vimy bomber. Royce had especially designed the Eagle so that it could continue to run even when parts of it had been shot away and a host of English lives were saved by his skill. German lives profited less: the Eagle made possible seven-hour flights to bomb Rhineland munition factories. In June 1917, however, the Germans bombed London, hitting Liverpool Street Station and killing 150 people. One would have thought that a nation accustomed to news of casualties such as 19,000 killed in a single day on the Somme could have sustained this relatively minor damage without too much difficulty, but there was an immediate and horrified outcry for vengeance.

The Government ordered from Rolls-Royce a new 600 h.p. engine (later called the Condor) to be used in the Handley-Page V/1500 bomber which was intended to bomb Berlin. This engine was tested in August 1918, but the war ended before its purpose could be carried into effect. Other engines made by Rolls-Royce in the First World War were the 75 h.p. Hawk, used in Blimps, and the Falcon for the Bristol fighter. Altogether Rolls-Royce provided seventy per cent of the aero-engines (and a total of over a million horsepower) used in British aircraft in the First World War, including 4,000 Eagles. The men who depended on these engines became as enamoured of Rolls-Royce as those who drove the armoured cars, as the following letter, written to the *Daily Mail* after the war, testifies:

Sir,

I note that the Rolls-Royce aero-engine department may be closed down if orders are not forthcoming. This, I think, explains our position today more clearly than anything else.

I well remember the hundreds of hours flown over the North Sea in twin-engined *land* machines fitted with Rolls-Royce engines, and although we were often out of sight of land while hunting for submarines we were never in danger with engine trouble.

In fact, the squadron never lost one machine through this cause. Can any other engine show such a record?

To all old R.A.F. pilots it seems unbelievable that the good old 'Rolls' is in danger of being scrapped.

PILOT.

None the less there was a degree of coolness in some of the company's relations with the Government. To increase the production of the Eagle the Ministry of Munitions wanted to create some more factories where the engine could be made. Johnson argued that it was more sensible to subcontract the production of parts out to other firms and so keep the number of central factories to a minimum; in this way it would not be necessary to instruct men in a factory in the manufacture of more than the particular part in which they specialised. This wrangle went on for two years before the Government conceded the point.

Rolls-Royce were also continually in trouble over the delivery of Eagles, because they had at once to make new engines and repair old ones in the same factory. Eventually Rolls-Royce were given the Clement-Talbot motor works in west London's Barlby Road for repair work. But the arguments had left a bitter taste so that 'C.J.' was conspicuously absent from the honours lists after the war. With Lloyd George using the honours system to line his pockets, however, there was no disgrace in that.

Johnson died in 1926, having been Managing Director (at first jointly with Rolls) since the beginning of the company. More than either Rolls or Royce he had created the company's public image by his discreetly clamorous proclamation of its cars' excellence before the First World War. Royce built the car and formed the traditions; Johnson built the legend and formed the distinctive Rolls-Royce public personality. The tinge of arrogance, the sometimes infuriating assumption of superiority, the lofty disdain of competitors – all of these characteristics (which people pretend to hate but secretly admire) stem from 'C.J.'s' approach. It is, however, only fair to remember that, at least in 'C.J.'s' time, this supremacy existed in reality as much as in his publicity; indeed, the basis of this publicity was simply to draw the public's attention to fact. Moreover this external reputation for supreme excellence, which Johnson fostered, has had a wholly beneficial effect on internal standards and morale. The two have fed on each other; some would say beyond the point of satiety.

Not that Johnson concentrated only on the company's external image; very much to the contrary. Both Rolls and Johnson recognised the importance of good works relations. At the opening of the Derby factory Rolls said:

'To produce the most perfect cars, you must have the most perfect
workmen; and having got these workmen it is our aim to educate
them up so that each man in these works can do his particular work
better than anyone else in the world.'

Such a policy has persisted to the present day. There is, though,
something a little overwhelming in some of the methods adopted
to achieve these praiseworthy ideals. Notices used to be hung up
in the Derby factory bearing the legends 'Be accurate', 'Be certain', or (most insidiously demanding of all) 'You are on your
honour not to depart from standards'. 'C.J.' also arranged for
badges of merit to be given to the workers demonstrating most
devotion to their task, a practice in which he thus preceded
Communist Russia.

Paternalism, though, also brings benefits if honestly adminis-
tered and Johnson, although his methods seem outdated, really
did have the welfare of the Rolls-Royce workers constantly in
mind. He used to arrange for the whole works staff to go to the
theatre on Monday nights. (Were they, one wonders, allowed to
opt out?) He organised regular medical checks and encouraged
all sporting activities. He ordered the odd day's holiday to cele-
brate a company triumph. Such gestures were not only evidence
of a genuine concern – they paid rich dividends in the loyalty
Rolls-Royce workers felt towards the firm. Royce could inspire
respect for his amazing skills, but was too narrowly concentrated
on his own tasks to handle works relations with the same thought-
fulness as Johnson.

Another of 'C.J.'s' characteristics was his instinctive knack of
judging what the potential Rolls-Royce buyer wanted and then
providing it. The one-car policy decision that made possible all
the pre-1914 triumphs is the most important example of his good
judgment. Another is his decision to retain the famous radiator.
Like those of the Parthenon the columns of the Rolls-Royce
radiator are slightly curved to give the illusion of straightness.
Moreover the design cannot be produced by machine, and the
welding of the sharp corners presents great difficulty. Nor after all
this trouble is it even particularly efficient; Royce wanted to scrap
it. But Johnson understood that the radiator was far too valuable
as a permanent symbol of Rolls-Royce, linking every new model
to the achievements of the past, to be discarded merely on grounds
of efficiency. He carried his point, and the radiator, albeit scaled
down in size, still crowns the latest Silver Shadow. The million-
aire, Nubar Gulbenkian, once ordered a Rolls without the
Rolls-Royce radiator and (though beauty is always in the eye of
the beholder) convincingly demonstrated the correctness of
Johnson's decision. Johnson was similarly at odds with Royce on
the question of how many gears the car should have. Royce always considered that a three-speed gearbox was perfectly sufficient. Johnson agreed but saw that even though many motorists
of those days only used two gears, they still enjoyed the com-

(ABOVE) A 1904 pre-Rolls, two-cylinder, Royce car – one of his earliest models.
(Photo: Rolls-Royce Ltd.)

(BELOW) One of the first 10 h.p. cars produced by Royce in the same year for the Hon. C. S. Rolls. A similar car was shown at the Paris Exhibition at the end of 1904. The key difference between the two models lies in the second car's familiar radiator, which is still retained in all Rolls-Royce cars. Royce was later prevented from modernising the radiator's design by Claude Johnson, who recognised its prestige value.
(Photo: Mansell Collection)

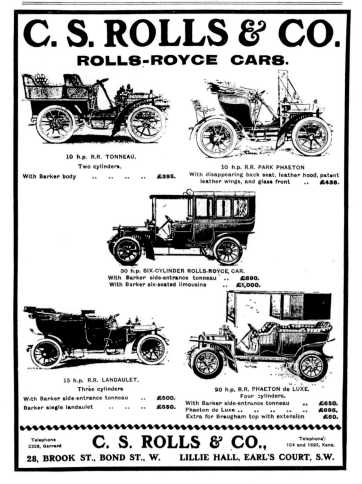

A very early advertisement issued in 1904 – the year that Henry Royce agreed to produce cars for the Hon. C. S. Rolls to market. The bodywork is still very much indebted to the influence of the horse-drawn carriage (note the footman's "disappearing back seat" in the second model).

(Photo: Autocar)

(ABOVE) The Hon. C. S. Rolls at Bournemouth, ready for take-off on the flight that killed him in July 1910. *(Photo: Mansell Collection)*

(BELOW) The famous flying Wright brothers sample the most luxurious form of land travel. *(Photo: Mansell Collection)*

"Wedding Bells", an ancestress of the tank. She saw active service in India and Afghanistan from 1915 to 1940 – as part time armoured, part time bridal car. Although armour plating added some 3 tons' weight to such cars, the Rolls-Royce engine needed only minor conversions. Despite the fact that the radiator did tend to boil occasionally, when those doors in front were shut, and that her driver's vision was restricted to a mere slit, she proved a formidable defence ally.

(*Photo: Rolls-Royce Ltd.*)

(ABOVE) Rolls-Royce engines powered the winning Schneider Trophy planes in 1929 and 1931. Collaboration with the Supermarine Company – the air-frame builders – led to the development of the Spitfire. *(Photo: Flight International)*

(BELOW) The Spitfire, mechanical hero of the Battle of Britain. The fact that German planes were just as efficient at the beginning of the Second World War added exertion to Rolls-Royce's efforts with the plane's Merlin engine. Its horse-power more than doubled during the course of the War. *(Photo: Flight International)*

(ABOVE) The "Flying Bedstead", displayed in 1954 – a debutante in vertical take-off.
(Photo: Flight)

(BELOW) A rather more svelte younger sister, the vertical take-off Hawker Siddeley Harrier.
(Photo: Flight)

(ABOVE) 1971 saw a new return to the traditions of elegant coachwork after the comparative ponderousness of the thirties and onwards. The Rolls-Royce Silver Shadow and Bentley T. series saloon – a business asset at around £12,000?

(Photo: Rolls-Royce Ltd.)

(OVERLEAF: ABOVE) Premature optimism over the 1968 signing of the ill-fated Lockheed contract. (Left) David Huddie, then managing director of Rolls-Royce, and (right) Lockheed's chairman, Daniel Haughton. *(Photo: Associated Press)*

(OVERLEAF: BELOW) More than 600 Rolls-Royce workers, in the shadow of unemployment, travelled from Derby for a mass lobby at the House of Commons on February 11th, 1971, before the nationalisation debate. *(Photo: Thomson Newspapers Ltd.)*

fortable knowledge that there were four available. This attitude is
amusingly caricatured by Bird and Hallows: 'I'll be damned if I'll
use four gears but I'll be doubly damned if I'll let you fob me off
with any fewer.' As with the radiator, Johnson's view prevailed.

'C.J.' had a well-earned reputation as an organisation master-
mind. Sometimes, though, he could overdo things, particularly
when his obsession with secrecy was aroused. When the prototype Phantom I appeared he sought to conceal its identity with the
code-name E.A.C. – Eastern Armoured Cars. As a purely corro-
borative detail designed to give artistic verisimilitude to this
camouflage, sheets of armour plating were left around the factory,
painted 'E.A.C.' in large white letters in case anyone missed the
point. Every driver of the car had to sign a paper in which he
undertook never to stop within sight of anyone.

The greatest of Johnson's works was that his solicitous attention, entailing the complete sacrifice of his own needs and cares,
very possibly saved Royce from death at a time when, though few
could have believed it of the creator of the Silver Ghost, his
greatest achievements still lay in the future. A generous action is
an easy enough accomplishment in prospect, but to be able to
sustain the good impulse in action over a long period, as Johnson
did in taking Royce abroad, argues a rare nature. Royce was a
great engineer, but one suspects that Johnson could have found
travelling companions more agreeable to his own tastes, which
were far more eclectic than those of either Rolls or Royce. He
was passionately fond of music, art and literature, yet his 'duty'
to Rolls-Royce always came first, to such an extent that few of his
working colleagues had any notion of his possessing any artistic
leanings.

> 'It was a great temptation to see you during my visit to Paris,' he
> wrote to a musical friend, 'but I had affairs of great importance to
> deal with and I resolved that I would sacrifice all my natural wishes
> to see you and your relations in order to devote myself with single-
> ness of mind to my duty.'

So single-minded was this devotion that in Rolls-Royce history only the image of the master organiser appears. And perhaps an organisation man is best judged by the cold statistics of
what was achieved. In 1905 the capital of Royce's at Manchester
was just over £100,000; by 1926 the Rolls-Royce capital amount-
ed to £814,000. But the increase in the profit on this capital is
more striking: in 1905 profits were £5,390 (or approximately five
per cent of capital); by 1913 they had swelled to £91,000 and by
1926 to £164,000 (or nearly twenty per cent of capital employed).
So 'C.J.' had presided over a period in which Rolls-Royce's
profitability ratio increased fourfold. There were critics after the
First War who claimed that he was out of touch with the revolutionary methods of mass manufacture which Henry Ford pioneered in the U.S. But as F. E. Smith remarked:

'Ford and the world Fords with you
Rolls and you Rolls alone.'

Johnson was incontestably the most important figure after Royce in the early history of the company. But could 'Johnson-Royce' ever have acquired the same associations, or slipped off the tongue with such aristocratic ease, as 'Rolls-Royce'?

III

Although he lived for twenty-three more years after his breakdown in 1911, years in which he did his most important work, Henry Royce's health never totally recovered. His exact illness is hard to discover: there is mention of intestinal disorder and of a malignant tumour. Just as he appeared to have recovered from the first attack he again collapsed at Le Canadel and had to be rushed back to England (Claude Johnson of course organising everything) for a serious operation. As the Silver Ghost bearing its stricken creator hurried across France it was overtaken by another big car and Royce, even at this moment alarmed that a competitor should produce a faster car, raised himself to see what make it was that had dared such presumption. He sank back in relief. 'It's all right,' he said, 'it's one of ours.' (In the First War, incidentally, many others besides Royce owed their lives to the Silver Ghost in ambulance conversion).

It has been suggested that Royce's removal from Derby to other places where his talent was still available, but at arm's length, was a blessing in disguise for Rolls-Royce. Had he remained on the spot in Derby his obsession with perfection in every tiny detail might well have over-run the bounds of commercial viability. Even as things were he would sometimes concentrate on developing a component to his own unmatchable standards before it had been properly established that this component was in fact to be used. Or he would become absorbed in relatively trivial details. He insisted, for example, on designing the tool kit for Rolls-Royces and the talent which had created the Eagle would address itself with equal energy to the problem of the correct shape for spanners. He had a horror of the adjustable variety and began by designing a full range of double-ended open spanners. But these could not satisfy him because each different size of nut requires a different degree of leverage to tighten it. He therefore designed a set of spanners with single ends and with the length of each spanner exactly appropriate for the size of nut.

Such an example provides a good illustration of Royce's methods because it is easily comprehensible to the mechanical layman. The difficulty of writing about Royce is that his life was devoted to matters technically so complex that a proper understanding of his contributions would require a three-year mechanics degree. It is possible, however, to grasp the character of his methods indirectly through anecdotes of his life outside Rolls-Royce. In small things are great talents revealed.

For instance, when Royce engaged a cook he had a stock test to enable him to make a snap judgment on her efficiency. She would be given some potatoes and told to boil them. Not, one would think, particularly difficult. But Royce knew that the time it takes to cook a potato perfectly depends on its size; and if the cook did not make allowance for this either by separating the larger from the smaller or by leaving the larger to boil for longer, her chances of employment were slim.

Everything mechanical fascinated him. In a London restaurant a waiter approaching him with a creaking trolley found a new design for the wheels sketched on the back of the menu. Once the sound of the vicar's distant but erring lawn mower so offended him that the cleric, hitherto ignorant of its faults, received lengthy instructions for its repair. He was not able, however, to render any reciprocal service; Royce's views on religion were brief and to the point: 'You can't be an engineer and still go to church.' Very likely it irked him that the mysteries of the universe were not susceptible of practical experiment. His mind rejected any imaginative speculation. Going to the moon?

'All nonsense' was the verdict. 'Even if they got there how would they get back? Start sinking wells for petrol I suppose, or waiting for a miracle. Man must keep to his own planet. He couldn't live on any other so what is the good of discussing corpses? I have no time for it myself. And I don't want to read such nonsense either.'

Much better to employ his minimal spare time designing a new pair of fire-tongs or a dog kennel for his adored labrador, or even a pigsty.

Is a man fortunate if he possesses one supreme talent which dwarfs the rest of his life? Royce was not a wholly narrow man; he had some interests outside engineering. He loved gardening and as far back as his Manchester days would rig up electric lights to enable him to pursue this absorbing interest at night. It was exactly designed to appeal to his temperament; it demanded patient, efficient labour and it was productive. He tried painting and was interested in astronomy. But for mere pleasure he had a puritanical distaste. Golf and tennis he regarded as a senseless, even a slightly immoral, waste of time. Rather than allow Rolls-Royce employees who came to visit him at Le Canadel to enjoy the delights of the Riviera, he would set them to work collecting fir cones. Farming, though, appealed to him for the same reasons as gardening, and in his last years he achieved considerable success with his crops.

But his interests were always peripheral to the central passion of his life; nothing ever really counted except his work. This monstrous appetite for labour which created such perfect machines for Rolls-Royce was, however, gorged at a high cost. His marriage, for instance, did not survive the intense efforts of the early days of Rolls-Royce.

Even his choice of wife could be seen to indicate a lack of imagination (or perhaps lack of interest), for he had been married at the same time as his partner Claremont and to the sister of Claremont's bride. It appears that there was no dramatic row, just a growing realisation of the impossibility of living with a man who gave twenty hours a day to his work. Royce always remained on friendly terms with his wife and provided for her generously in his will. There were no children. He was fortunate to acquire a devoted companion in Nurse Aubin, who undoubtedly prolonged his life by the care she lavished on him during his last twenty years.

Royce hated showiness in design and people alike, and, for all his confidence in his skills, was himself the most modest of men. 'Henry Royce, mechanic' he once wrote in a child's autograph book. He recoiled sharply from any public acclaim:

> 'I do not wish the statue the Directors so kindly voted should be made of me to be erected in a public place, especially while I am alive . . . it was not my wish that it should be made, and I can only suggest that it should be erected at the Works. I do not like Mr. Claremont's inscription, and much prefer your own, but this should be shortened everywhere possible.'

The editor of *Who's Who* was deliciously rebuked:

> 'I do not think it would make any real difference to the Company whether my name is in *Who's Who* or not, and while thanking you very much for your kind offer of looking over the suggestions, I have decided to do nothing at present on the matter.'

A journalist once asked him what would happen if his designs were leaked to rivals.

> 'Oh, I don't think it would matter very much,' came the reply. 'What I mean by that is this: you may design an engine, but after that you have got to find the men who can make it. The design of this engine is really quite simple, but only the finest engineers could make it effective.'

There was no especial virtue in his particular talent; all good work was excellent. He even took the trouble to instruct a sweeper in the proper method of using his brush, for, he insisted, 'the humblest thing which is done correctly is noble'. (Eric Gill, the sculptor, thought that sentence so well summed up Royce's philosophy that he carved it above his mantelpiece. The effect was rather spoilt, however, by the pretentious use of Latin, of which Royce had no knowledge).

The end came in 1933. 'I know that I am dying, but please let there be no trouble about it for anybody.' He had created new standards in engineering and left behind the men and the organisation that have sought to carry on his traditions to the present day. Rolls was still very recognisably Royce's to the last day of the company. But he did not satisfy himself anymore than did his

engines. 'I have only one regret' he said as he lay dying 'that I have
not worked harder.'

IV

Excellence is always apt to create enemies and Rolls-Royce have
never been without detractors. In part they have themselves to
blame; by their claim, indeed assumption, that their cars are and
always have been the best in the world they have invited critics to
apply higher standards in judging Rolls-Royces than other
makes. If there is a car faster than the Rolls-Royce, there will always be someone to denounce the Rolls-Royce as sluggish; if a
tiny creak is heard from the coachwork then the car is deemed to
rattle like a tin can. Moreover, there is something about Rolls-
Royces, perhaps the ignorant adulation which the name itself
inspires, or possibly just the impossibility of affording the price,
that arouses the most cantankerous strain in some motoring
connoisseurs. To experts in any field there is always something
rather aggravating in the recognition that although the ignorant
populace know one hundredth as much as themselves about a
particular subject they derive quite as much pleasure from it.

And so even the Silver Ghost did not escape a few knowledge-
able sneers. The engine was described as 'a triumph of workmanship over design', while another common criticism was 'Ah
yes, wonderful car – if you can afford to use thirty horse-power to
silence the fifteen that do the work'. The Silver Ghost, production
of which was resumed after the war and continued for another
seven years, did perhaps outlive its time. By the mid-1920s the
Hispano-Suiza was certainly a more advanced car technically,
v. hile in England the Lanchester 40 was a dangerous rival. Yet the
Ghost continued to sell until the very end, both in England and
America.

Another instance – from a later period – of the critics' willing-
ness to pounce on Rolls-Royce occurred when the German
autobahnen were opened. The company issued a sensible warning
to Rolls-Royce drivers that they should not flog the engines
mercilessly at the highest speeds for long periods; but this was
interpreted by some who should have known better (and probably did) as a confession of a lack of confidence felt in their engines by Rolls-Royce.

Yet the critics sometimes had a point. The company was un-
deniably slow about incorporating the latest technical advances
into their cars. Whereas electric lighting and starters had become
standard equipment on Cadillacs in 1912 (and on other models
soon after) they remained an optional extra on the Silver Ghost
until after the First War. In view of Royce's early electrical skill
this is rather surprising.

Again, Rolls-Royce were late in fitting four-wheel brakes, a bad lapse considering the huge weights of their cars. The leaders in this respect were Hispano-Suiza and Rolls-Royce (pursuing a well-established company policy with regard to rivals) bought a Hispano-Suiza to discover how its complicated braking system worked. Royce duly designed a modified version, but the first application in testing well justified his faith in the value of practical experiment. In 'Silver Ghosts and Silver Dawn', a book chockfull of interesting Rolls-Royce reminiscences, W. A. Robotham describes the first trial of the new brakes:

> 'At about 7 o'clock on a spring evening we drove out of the works gate in the dusk without attracting any attention . . . and proceeded about 400 yards to the T-junction where there is a main road. Here, Hives gently applied the brakes – with the most astonishing results. There was a shattering clatter from the front axle which shook the chassis from stem to stern so violently that both the headlamp bulbs disintegrated, leaving us in the gloom with wing lamps only. By this time the car was moving only at a walking pace, and Hives brought it to rest on the handbrake. He was obviously as dumbfounded as I was, and after a short pause, said "What a hell of a row! Let's get it home to the factory before we're arrested." We thereupon crept furtively back to the experimental department.'

Eventually Royce and his team ironed out the difficulties and the brakes were standard on all models from 1924.

Independent front suspension was another development which Rolls-Royce were slow to adopt. This time the model was provided by General Motors. Of course Rolls-Royce always had a ready answer to criticism: that they were not going to incorporate any new system on *their* cars until they had thoroughly convinced themselves that it had been brought to the highest possible pitch of perfection. But this stock riposte was not always convincing.

The first new model produced after the war was the Twenty, with which Rolls-Royce in 1922 returned to the smaller car market. Social convention of the time meant that a big luxury car like the Silver Ghost was invariably chauffeur-driven; but the Twenty was designed to appeal to the proliferating numbers of owner-drivers. Standards of workmanship in the new car, however, were high as ever. The Twenty acquired the reputation of being a sluggard, but this was unjust since it could reach 60 m.p.h. (the limit, it may be recalled, was still 20 m.p.h.). The real trouble was that in those times one of the main attractions of a Rolls-Royce, appealing powerfully to contemporary drivers new to motoring and scared stiff of the next gear change, was the old story that it would operate in top gear only. This was true enough of the Silver Ghost but less so of the Twenty, although its engine was still marvellously flexible. Anyway, the Twenty slowly grew up, becoming the 20/25 in 1929, the 25/30 in 1936 and finally developing into the Wraith in 1938.

The reign of the Silver Ghost, meanwhile, had finally ended in 1925.

'After seven years of experiment and test,' the company announced, 'the 40/50 h.p. six-cylinder Phantom chassis emerged, and is offered to the public as the most suitable type possible for a mechanical carriage under present day conditions.'

The public had, however, to be able to fork out between £2,500 and £3,000 in order to avail themselves of this offer. (The chassis by itself cost £1,900). The Phantom I was produced for only four years and never quite recaptured the first fine careless rapture of the Silver Ghost. Indeed, after the First World War the Rolls-Royce image solidified, as though with the coming of middle age. There was no more youthful cavorting in Tourist Trophies and the like; during these latter days the cars were moving amongst royalty and were perhaps becoming a little overconscious of the fact. Despite a huge 100 h.p. engine which could provide thirty-three per cent more power than that of the Ghost at full stretch, and a maximum speed of seventy-five to eighty m.p.h., the Phantom I's great weight (nearly three tons) made it less attractive to drive, and somehow more inclined to make the passengers sick. Some extraordinary attempts were made to hot up the engine; such as Amherst Villiers's who, in 1927, supercharged a Phantom I, using an Austin 7 engine to drive the blower.

In 1929 Phantom I gave way to Phantom II, which has found more favour with motoring experts. The engine was basically the same as its predecessor's (only with twenty-five per cent more power) but the chassis was entirely new, being lighter and considerably stiffened. The 'Continental' Phantom II with a hotted engine is one of the finest, perhaps *the* finest, model Rolls-Royce ever produced. The Phantom III was the first car to appear (in 1936) without Royce's involvement. Powered by what was almost a miniature aircraft engine (12 cylinder Vee formation) this last pre-World War Two Phantom could easily do 100 m.p.h. and was often fitted with fabulously luxurious coachwork. The cost was £4,000. Still, in those days, petrol was only 1s. 5d. (7p) a gallon.

The saddest motoring casualty of the Depression years was Bentley's, which Rolls-Royce bought up in 1931. This seemed a strange liaison at the time, a case of beauty and the beast. But the Bentley was a noble, powerful and magnificently untamed beast, which had won at Le Mans four years running. Bentley drivers were devoted enthusiasts, the kind who find it better to travel noisily than to arrive. What they thought of Rolls-Royce's ideals of silence and reliability can easily be imagined, less easily printed. None the less, once they had recovered from the horror of not being deafened by their car, they were bound to admit that the $3\frac{1}{2}$ litre Rolls-Bentley (after 1936 $4\frac{1}{4}$ litres) had a very considerable performance. E. R. Hall drove this car with notable success at Ards in the three years 1934 to 1936. It is a pity that the Bentley sports car tradition has not been followed through in recent years.

The great economic depression of the late Twenties and early Thirties hit Rolls-Royce themselves. Between the wars they had established a subsidiary company in America to exploit further what had always been a good market for its cars. In 1919 there was available in America a pool of suitable labour which had been trained by Rolls-Royce technicians to make aero-engines during the war; further, Claude Johnson wanted to circumvent the high American tariff barriers. The arguments were so strong they demanded action and in November 1919 Rolls-Royce, America opened at Springfield, Massachussetts.

This company produced a total of 2,944 cars in ten years, (1,703 Silver Ghosts and 1,241 Phantom Is). All the parts were made in America except for the crankshafts, the wheels and some of the electrical equipment. Every effort was made to ensure that the American version matched up to Derby standards; indeed, the odd Derby chassis was intermingled with the American output to give each customer the chance that his was 'ye genuine olde English Rolls-Royce'. Still further, to instil this uplifting feeling the first models were made with right-hand drive, surely one of the most extraordinary commercial decisions ever made. It seemed to work, though; at first the new company prospered, building up its output to four hundred cars in 1928. When the Derby factory switched to Phantom IIs, however, the Americans naturally preferred this more advanced model to the Phantom Is from Springfield. With the Great Depression beginning to lower over the economy, there was not the capital available to finance the extensive retooling required to produce Phantom IIs at Springfield; at the same time, of course, the demand for expensive luxury cars dropped sharply. The result was that production tailed off to a dribble; the company never recovered and was declared bankrupt in 1934. But if the Depression had not come at such a particularly awkward moment there might well be a Rolls-Royce America today – possibly even competing with the American giants in the manufacture of aero-engines. In the Second World War at least the plant would certainly have been turned over to aero-engine manufacture.

The coachbuilder Brewster made some glorious bodies for the American Rolls-Royces, at once distinctively American and unmistakeably Rolls-Royce. In England too the post-1918 years produced stunningly beautiful Rolls-Royce cars; whatever the Phantom I's defects the looks of some versions more than compensate. Best of all perhaps is the Phantom II Continental; only the dignity of the radiator prevents it from being labelled rakish. These things are all a matter of fashion and personal taste but to the writer it seems that, from the mid-1930s on, the designs tend to become too ponderously pre-occupied with their own gravity, and for the first time it becomes obvious why a Rolls-Royce is a natural choice for funerals, or indeed, weddings. (Incidentally that brings to mind the story of the Scottish Co-op who rather puzzled Rolls-Royce by ordering thirty limousines and five chassis, with an especial request to omit the radios and heaters – which came included in the price – and give a rebate instead. The point was queried and the reply came that the radios and heaters were not needed because 'our customers will only take one ride in these vehicles'. They were intended for hearses. In 1961 the Scottish Co-op had the largest Rolls-Royce fleet in the world, 240 cars employed almost entirely for weddings and funerals).

The latest Silver Shadow marks a return to a sleeker line, though the advertising, necessarily in days when it is often the company rather than the individual who pays, has become un-worthily vulgar. Most Silver Shadow owners, it appears, regard the car as a valuable business asset. At £12,000 an asset, one begins to appreciate why all is not well with British business. In 1905, by contrast, it had been to doctors that Rolls-Royce had urged us to turn for advice about cars:

> 'Doctors and others connected with the medical profession have, after trying the leading makes, declared the Rolls-Royce to be the only petrol car which they could bring up to a patient's house and drive away without the possibility of disturbing the patient.'

But some Rolls-Royces there be which have no memorial, which have perished as though they had never been. Over the years, Rolls-Royce have made many prototypes which for one reason or another have never been developed into production models. They may have been great cars, but simply not in line with the company policy at a particular moment. The cause allows of no reprieve – the penalty for non-production is ever the same: annihilation. The men who made them systematically dismember and destroy them.

An admirer once asked Royce what would happen if Rolls-Royce ever produced a bad car. 'Madam,' he replied, 'the man on the gate would not let it out of the works.' Today there is still the same ruthless insistence on testing each and every part. Indeed, more sophisticated versions of mechanical torture have been devised. There is a steering test machine, which throws the wheels continuously from lock to lock against concrete kerb stones. And all new components have to survive 300 hours on a special chassis which, Bird and Hallows report:

> 'Simulates the effect of driving the complete chassis, loaded with ¾ ton of ballast, at 50 m.p.h. along a road with slightly rounded humps of concrete, six inches high, so staggered at four foot inter-vals that on and off side wheels take the blows alternately.'

Moreover there are fearsome tests on each individual car. Every engine undergoes a gruelling eight hours' session on a test-

ing rig fuelled by cooking gas, of which time 30 minutes is taken up
with idling, 30 minutes at medium revolutions and seven punish-
ing hours at full throttle. Every twentieth engine is completely
dismembered and each single part examined, many of them under
a microscope. If the slightest suspicion about any detail arises,
every one of the twenty engines in the batch is similarly stripped
and ruthlessly scrutinised in the minutest detail. Every fiftieth
engine to come off the assembly line is put through an even more
stringent twenty-four-hour running trial and examination; its
forty-nine predecessors meeting the same fate if any detail is
faulted. The rest of the car is examined with similar suspicion by
the testers. Sometimes a whole day's production – perhaps five
cars – is rejected. No wonder a former employee remarked that it
was surprising the cars had any life left in them when they reached the road.

Post-war Rolls-Royces have one threat that the Silver Ghosts
hardly ever did – that of rust. This has been due to a decline in
the quality of the iron available, particularly in the years immediately after the war. Rust of course is as corrosive to the Rolls-
Royce image as to the bodywork since it invalidates the claim
that cars last at least a lifetime. The difficulty has been tackled
with typical Rolls-Royce thoroughness as the publicity for the
Silver Shadow shows:

'Prevention of corrosion starts at the design stage where pockets in
the bodywork capable of harbouring dirt or damp are eliminated,
shielded or well-drained. Where risk of corrosion is severe, zinc-
coated sheet steel is specified instead of ordinary mild steel.
   Anti-corrosion treatment begins with meticulous cleaning of the
body shell.
   Then comes a seven-stage phosphate dip process which gives a
chemical change to the surface of the metal and makes it very
resistant to corrosion. After a coat of acid-etch primer, the body
shell is immersed in primer which is baked on. Two thick coats of
filler follow before seventy pounds of underseal is applied. Then
more primer followed by three coats of coloured paint. Only after
the car has been built and road-tested are the top coats sprayed
on and the finishing processes completed. In all about fourteen coats
of primer, filler and paint will have been applied.'

What will become of such fanatically meticulous methods when
the car section of the company becomes the responsibility of new
owners? Surely only the Rolls-Royce traditions of perfection
could ensure the continued maintenance of standards as demanding; and they are traditions which would give any profit-
orientated managerial whizz-kid a nightmare. When Lord
Beaverbrook gained financial control of the company, immediately after the First World War he tried vainly to persuade the directors to modify their methods and introduce some of the mass
production techniques that Ford were using in America. The
threat the Rolls-Royce traditions now face is far more serious.

Yet the new owner should remember that these methods *do* pay. Rolls-Royce now produce more than 2,000 cars a year and notwithstanding the price there is a demand for more. But, as the man at Rolls-Royce superciliously remarked to *The Times*: 'I hate to say this, but a Rolls-Royce made by anybody else just wouldn't be a Rolls-Royce, would it?'

It might seem that my concentration on cars has been out of proportion, since this part of the company has in recent years been a tiny enterprise beside the mammoth aero-engine business. But that is not how the company sees it. In 1961 Sir Denning Pearson, Chairman of Rolls-Royce, told *The Sunday Telegraph:*

> 'All of us have our roots in the motor car division – the company started on wheels and we take a tremendous interest in the car, keeping it mechanically up to date. Oh no, it is certainly not a question of the tail wagging the dog. In the public mind the company's name is still associated with the motor car.'

The car, in fact, is the source of the legend, and the legend will not be quickly forgotten. And all the stories, many of them myth, will live on. It is said, for example, that the Rolls-Royce badge, formerly red, became black when Henry Royce died in 1933. Some Rolls-Royce people stoutly deny this relation of cause and effect but the fact remains that the badge *did* change colour at about that time. What of the rumour that the Silver Lady mascot on top of the radiator was made of solid silver? There were certainly enough people who believed this, with the result that it became rash to leave the lady unchaperoned. Many owners, including the Duke of Edinburgh, took her off the radiator and kept her safely under lock and key. The original of this figure was commissioned by Lord Montagu from Charles Sykes, R.A. in 1911; Lord Montagu's secretary (who was tragically drowned in the war), posed as the model. It was Claude Johnson who adopted the statuette as a model for all subsequent cars. The nymph recently underwent an undignified metamorphosis into plastic to satisfy American public safety demands.

Equally, there will always be those who believe Rolls-Royces are guaranteed for life (actually only for three years), and that they are hand made (totally impossible). There are some stories, though, which one would dearly like to believe, like that of the visitor being escorted round the Rolls-Royce factory who said to his guide: 'Let's see the cars running – start them up.' 'The engines are already running, Sir' was the inevitable reply. Perhaps the most famous story of all is the one about the Rolls-Royce which was taken touring in Switzerland and on a mountainous road had the misfortune to break a spring. The owner limped to the nearest town and there telephoned Rolls-Royce in London. The next day the Rolls-Royce agent appeared with a spare that had been flown out and the trip was completed without further incident. Back in England the owner awaited the bill and when it did not arrive telephoned the company, gave all the particulars and queried the non-arrival. After a few minutes holding on, back came the majestic reply: 'Sir, there is no such thing as a broken spring on a Rolls-Royce.'

V

After 1918 it was by no means a foregone conclusion that the aero-engine part of the company would survive – in spite of the contribution it had made in the war. Clearly the demand from the R.A.F., to which it wholly owed its existence, would fall off considerably. On the other hand the beginnings of commercial flying offered hope for the future. In 1919 the first regular flights between London and Paris were inaugurated, all the aircraft operating the service using Rolls-Royce Eagle engines. The fare was 15 guineas so at least some things have become cheaper in the last fifty years.

There were, however, more exciting things happening in the flying world of 1919. The *Daily Mail* prize of £10,000, offered in 1913, for the first transatlantic flight was still unclaimed and, the end of the war having somewhat restricted the opportunities open to those who enjoyed hazarding their lives, there was no shortage of contestants for the prize. The victory, in 1919, of John Alcock and Arthur Whitten Brown was rightly claimed by Claude Johnson as a triumph for Rolls-Royce since the two 350 h.p. Eagle engines had hummed steadily away throughout the sixteen-hour flight – one of the few factors in the perilous journey not to cause anxiety. Less publicised by Rolls-Royce, however, was the fact that Hawker and Grieves, two other contestants, whose plane was also Eagle-powered, were forced to plunge down into the Atlantic through overheating in the engine. Fortunately they had managed to keep going long enough to find a ship near which to splash down; the Royal telegram of condolence that had been sent to their wives was happily premature. Other epic flights of those days involving Rolls-Royce engines included that of the Smith brothers from England to Australia, completed in 124 hours flying time; and the first England-India flight. 'Excellent as the machine is' commented General Salmond of the Handley Page bi-plane used on the India journey 'the Rolls-Royce engines were, to a very great extent, responsible for the success of the flight.'

There were more encomia for Rolls-Royce from the explorer Roald Amundsen, who, not content with having beaten Scott to the Pole in 1911, planned in 1925 to reach the same spot by air. Two Dornier monoplane flying-boats, with the inevitable Eagle engines, were chosen for the flight, each plane to carry a crew of three. Amundsen's plan was that if the petrol that could be carried turned out to be insufficient for both return flights, one flying-boat could be jettisoned and the petrol remaining in it transferred to the other, in which all six could then return. The idea that the Arctic regions might not provide ideal, or even possible, landing and take-off areas did not seem to occur to him, or if it did he suppressed the unwelcome thought. The initial take-off was from ice – the first time a flying-boat had used an ice runway to become airborne.

In the event the two flying-boats did have to crash-land, and the link-up of the two parties and the transference of petrol were only achieved by truly superhuman efforts. The exhausted, half-starved men struggled for twenty-six days to make a crude runway, and in the nick of time their faithful Eagle engines lifted them into the air as the ice melted and cracked away beneath them.

In these circumstances Amundsen's tribute – 'the regular beat of our two Rolls-Royce engines, which never varied in the slightest, and which might well be considered the height of perfection in British workmanship, gave one confidence' – seems less than adequate.

All these adventurous achievements were excellent publicity but could not disguise the fact that the years succeeding the First World War were bleak ones for the Rolls-Royce aero-engine section. It was entirely dependent on overhauling and supplying spare parts for the Eagles and Condors that were fast becoming obsolete. In these circumstances it was a bold move – and one that especially deserved to be remembered in 1971 – for the company, without any outside assistance, and with no certainty that it would recover its expenditure, to finance the development of a revolutionary new engine. This was the Kestrel, and since it was a direct ancestor of the Merlin which powered practically every British plane in the Second World War, the country has much for which to thank Rolls-Royce.

The effectiveness of an aircraft engine depends on producing the maximum possible power from the minimum possible weight and in this respect the Kestrel, which used special aluminium alloys developed by Rolls-Royce, provided a vital breakthrough. It was also the first Rolls-Royce engine to have the six cylinders of each of the two banks in one block, instead of separate individual cylinders as previously. The horse-power went up from about 500 in the earlier versions to 765 by the end of its development.

From the Kestrel were derived the engines which Rolls-Royce provided for Britain's Schneider Trophy air race triumphs in 1929 and 1931. Britain had also won the Trophy with a Napier engine in 1927 and the Supermarine Company asked Royce to develop another with which to defend the title. Because of uncertainties about whether the Air Ministry would in fact support this defence

Royce had only seven months in which to produce, test and instal his engine. He started with the Buzzard, a larger, 925 h.p. version of the Kestrel, and by the time of the race had managed to more than double its power to 1,900 h.p. This was perhaps his most remarkable achievement, though he would have been the first to insist on sharing the credit with his team.

Powered by this engine, the Supermarine S.6 easily won the Trophy, its speed of 328 m.p.h. being 44 m.p.h. faster than that of the second place. 'The Rolls-Royce racing engine managed to give off its 1,800 or so h.p. with surprisingly little fuss' *Flight* magazine rather coolly reported. Royce was given a baronetcy. The victory was repeated in 1931 but the lustre of this achievement was rather dimmed by the absence of any opposition. Even the British entry needed Lady Houston to save it; she guaranteed £100,000 towards the cost in order, as she put it, 'to prevent the Socialist Government being spoil sports.' Not even the Socialists could prevent the Supermarine raising the winning speed to 378 m.p.h. and within a few months it had cracked the 400 m.p.h. barrier for the first time. The real importance of the Schneider Trophy, however, was that the knowledge Rolls-Royce gained from developing the racing engines later bore fruit in the Merlin; and that it established the connection with the Supermarine Company (in particular with the designer, R. J. Mitchell) which subsequently produced the Spitfire. Anybody who saw Leslie Howard in the film 'The First of the Few' knows that.

The Schneider Trophy engines also found themselves on wheels and on water, where they were responsible for a remarkable series of speed records in the 1930s. Malcolm Campbell installed the engine in his Bluebird and successively beat the existing and then his own land records. By the mid thirties the five-ton car was hurtling along at 276 m.p.h. This was still a good way off the 300 m.p.h. on which Campbell had set his heart, and he went to Utah in 1935 to attempt this speed. On the first run a tyre burst but by a miracle both Campbell and the car survived; the next run achieved the target at 301 m.p.h. But by now George Eyston had hit on the sensible idea that two Rolls-Royce aircraft engines in a car must be better than one, and his colossal 4,000 h.p. Thunderbolt took the record to 357 m.p.h. After that, however, John Cobb managed to show that Rolls-Royce engines were not an indispensable precondition for breaking the land speed record.

VI

History provides a succession of great 'ifs', stretching from Cleopatra's nose to President Nixon's, and generally their consideration, although fascinating, is a singularly unprofitable occupation. But that this country could not have withstood the invasion of the sledge-hammering German armies in 1940, and that it was the Battle of Britain that prevented Hitler attaining the air superiority he needed before launching such an invasion, are postulations hardly susceptible of argument. If one then adds that it was the Spitfires and Hurricanes (and of course their pilots) that won the Battle of Britain and that these planes owed not only their power but their very existence to the Merlin engine, one has created a chain of very strong hypotheses linking our survival in 1940 to the achievement of Rolls-Royce.

It must be emphasised, moreover, that Rolls-Royce financed the early development of the Merlin, like that of the Kestrel, entirely from their own resources and at their own risk. It is of course true that the company did not suffer for this action – quite the reverse; but in 1932, when Private Venture (or P.V.) 12 – as the Merlin was originally named – was first launched, Rolls-Royce had no guarantee of the future Government orders.

That was just before Royce died, but he lived long enough to lay down the broad principles of design. After his death Elliot, for so long his assistant, became Chief Engineer, while at Derby Hives, true to the master's methods, systematically destroyed every part of the engine in order to discover its weaknesses. A notable feature was the glycol coolant adopted; the paradoxical advantage of which was that the engine could operate at almost double the temperatures normal until that time. This in turn meant a smaller radiator and less wind resistance.

P.V. 12 ran into a good many difficulties in the early stages of its development and it was not until October 1933 that the engine first ran, and April 1935 that the first flight, in a Hawker Hart bi-plane, took place. By the end of 1935 the Merlin Mark I was in production.

Meanwhile, Sydney Camm, the great aircraft designer, had heard about the power of the private venture Rolls-Royce engine and, starting from this fact, began to create a fighter of radically new design. This was to be the Hawker Hurricane, which shot down more German planes than the Spitfire in the Battle of Britain. At roughly the same time Mitchell, also with the Rolls-Royce engine very much in mind, was working on plans for the Spitfire; and the first prototype flew in early 1936.

It is an interesting if rather terrifying comment on the backwardness of Britain's air forces before these developments that, in order to obtain a suitably up-to-date monoplane in which to test their new engine, Rolls-Royce had to spend £13,000 on a German He.70. The Germans owed their lead in airframe design to the Treaty of Versailles which, by forbidding them to build powered aeroplanes, had forced them to concentrate on gliders. By the end of 1935, however, the British Government had woken up to the seriousness of the position sufficiently to place orders for 1,500 first line fighters.

The deteriorating international situation gradually made it

clear just how vital the Merlin was going to be and at Derby
Hives, now Works Manager at Rolls-Royce, made every effort to
concentrate the company's resources on the engine. The Government wanted to establish a series of 'shadow' factories, which
would make use of former car workers to produce the Merlin;
but just as Royce in 1914 could not stomach the thought of his
factory turning out engines of inferior design, so now Rolls-
Royce were anxious not to entrust the manufacture of their brainchild to alien hands. The Government, hardly being in a position
to argue, conceded the point and in the years before the war there
was a mushrooming of Rolls-Royce factories, Government-
financed in construction, but run entirely by the company. Truly
the Merlin rewarded the taking of the initial risk; the new plants
remained with Rolls-Royce after the war.

First the Derby works were increased from 803,500 to 1.2 million square feet; then in 1938 a Rolls-Royce factory appeared on
the unlikely site of the corporation rubbish dump at Crewe, and
so quickly that the first Merlin was produced there only eleven
months after building began. Finally Haldenby, the same man
who, as a young apprentice, had helped Royce build his first car,
supervised the construction of the Glasgow factory which
opened in 1940. The rapid training of labour was only possible
because Derby had so many highly skilled men that sufficient
numbers could be moved to Crewe and Glasgow to lead and instruct the new forces. 'Work till it hurts' said Hives, echoing
Royce. In the War Rolls-Royce certainly did that, an eighty-hour
week being common. Hives himself set the example, directing the
57,000 labour force (a third of whom were women), besides
being in charge of every aspect of the aero-engine business. By
1943 the Derby, Crewe and Glasgow factories were turning out
18,000 Merlins a year, compared with 2,000 in 1940.

In addition the pressure of events eventually forced the manufacture of Merlins by other companies, although Rolls-Royce
had to provide the training. Fords made 30,000 Merlins at Manchester and in America the Packhard company, which before the
war had created the Phantom III's chief rivals, produced a
slightly modified American version, the Merlin 28.

The Germans were naturally among the first to appreciate the
importance of the Rolls-Royce contribution to the Allies' cause.
In 1940 a German bomber formation was reported to be in
special training for the destruction of the Glasgow works, but
since only one bomb hit the Rolls-Royce factory there during the
entire course of the war, either the report or the celebrated
Teuton efficiency was singularly fallible. At Derby the main
works were carefully camouflaged and Rolls-Royce took over a
number of premises within a twenty-mile radius of the town in
order to duplicate certain key processes and thus minimise the
chance of a bad hit paralysing production. The Government also
provided especially strong anti-aircraft defences. In the event,

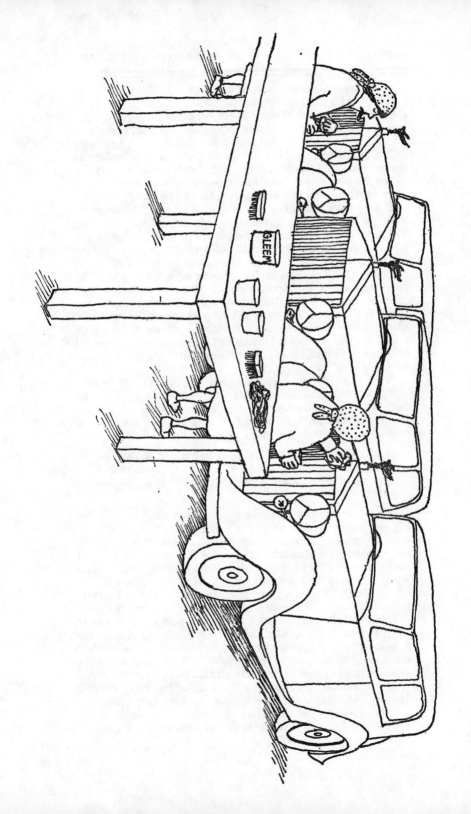

Rolls-Royce at Derby escaped as lightly as Rolls-Royce at
Glasgow, with just one hit, which did little damage. For some
extraordinary reason William Joyce, who as 'Lord Haw Haw'
broadcast German propaganda to England, sought to strike us
into dismay by announcing that 5,000 motor cycles had been
destroyed. He reckoned without the tough British fibre which was
able to take even this appalling intelligence with equanimity.

The Merlin, as has been said, powered almost every British
plane in the Second World War. But, the Spitfire having earned a
legendary reputation akin to that of Rolls-Royce, the engine is
most renowned for its association with this particular plane.
The fame of the Spitfire, however, is apt to obscure that, in the
first stages of the Battle of Britain, its performance was certainly
not superior to the German Messerschmitt 109. Failure to
recognise this fact deprives Rolls-Royce of much of the credit
due to them for the developments of the Merlin which they
effected during the war. Indeed, after the first six weeks of the
Battle of Britain the Germans had us trembling on the verge of a
defeat from which probably only Hitler's decision to switch his
attack to London from the vital airfields in the South of England
saved us. It is against this background that Rolls-Royce's contribution should be considered.

The R.A.F. lost many planes in the battle for France in May
and June 1940, but a German Me 190E was captured intact and
flown back to England for tests against the Spitfire. One of the
R.A.F. pilots who flew it recounts this incident in language
magnificently reminiscent of the period and of his calling:

> 'I remember all the boffins were there, and after their usual incom-
> prehensible nattering and zipping of high-speed operated slide rules,
> they decided that something had been established by George and
> me cavorting about in the sky.'

What was established was that the Messerschmitt had the
edge in both rate of climb and ceiling. But whereas the Messerschmitt performance did not develop at all in the course of the
war, Rolls-Royce were able to improve the Spitfire to such an
extent that by 1944 its rate of climb had almost doubled and its
speed increased by nearly 100 m.p.h. The horse-power of the
Merlin engine went up from 1,000 in 1939 to 2,100 in 1944.
Especially important, even before the end of the Battle of
Britain, Rolls-Royce had given the plane a performance at least
equal to that of the Messerschmitt, thus helping to provide the
opportunity, so magnificently seized by the R.A.F., of hauling
the country back from the precipice. Rolls-Royce engineers were
attached to every station so that they could learn the pilots' needs
at first hand and let Derby know exactly what was required.
Their wireless instructions to pilots were also immensely valuable
in helping stricken planes to land. Indeed, their expertise in this
respect was legendary: it was said that they could spot engine

trouble to the exact cylinder from a mile away.

The drama of the Battle of Britain always captures the limelight at the expense of the bombers. Yet, if the Spitfires staved
off defeat, the destruction wrought on Germany from the air
played an important part in the final victory. The outstanding
bomber of the war was the Lancaster; it first appeared in 1941
and by 1945 had dropped 608,600 tons of bombs. Its engines,
need it be said, were Merlins.

One of the reasons why the Allies' bombing was never decisive
before July 1944 was that they did not have the fighters with the
necessary range to give them air supremacy over Germany. The
Luftwaffe would hold off until the accompanying fighters had to
turn back and was then able to attack the defenceless bombers.

By these tactics the Germans inflicted terrible losses, particularly on the American Flying Fortresses which carried out day-
light raids. In October 1943 a force of 291 Flying Fortresses
attacked Schweinfurt; 60 did not return and 138 were badly
damaged. In these circumstances the advent of the American
Mustang, which was 70 m.p.h. faster than the German fighters
and which had a range long enough to enable it to reach and
return from the eastern limits of Germany from England, was a
vital breakthrough.

In prototype, the Mustang had been powered by an American
engine, but when the Merlin was substituted, the maximum speed
immediately increased by 80 m.p.h. to 450 m.p.h. and the production model was even faster. Some 14,000 Mustangs were
produced in six months after October 1943. When Goering saw
them escorting the Flying Fortresses over Berlin he admitted
that Germany had lost the war.

If the Merlin had never been developed . . . no, the conse-
quences are too unthinkable to contemplate. But at Derby they
played it cool. 'We're just ironmongers,' Hives insisted.

VII

The Merlin also went to war on the ground, installed in the
Cromwell and Challenger tanks. This conversion, rather like
trying to cram an elephant into a telephone box, was carried out
by Rolls-Royce's car division; all car production, of course,
having ceased on the outbreak of war.

Throughout the inter-war years Liddell Hart had vainly sought
to drum home to the War Office the vital importance of the tank
in modern warfare. The Germans, though, read his works
eagerly and put his ideas into practice with such effect that by
the end of 1940 their armies had conquered nearly the whole of
Europe. Liddell Hart had the painful satisfaction of being
justified by Hitler's successes in a war against his own country.

Despite the success of the very primitive tanks of the First World War, the British Army remained determinedly unconvinced about the effectiveness of the new weapon. In 1925 Field Marshal Haig, who throughout the First World War had fretted for the chance of a thumping good cavalry charge, gave his listeners the benefit of a lifetime's experience in matters military:

> 'Some enthusiasts today talk about the probability of the horse becoming extinct, and prophesy that the aeroplane, the tank and the motor car will supersede the horse in future wars . . . I feel sure that as time goes on, you will find just as much use for the horse – the well-bred horse – as you have ever done in the past.'

In 1929 the Army spent £607,000 on fodder for horses and £72,000 on petrol for tanks. And so, at the beginning of the war, Britain possessed only one reliable tank, the Vickers Valentine Mark I. Reliability was in fact its only asset, for its puny two-pounder guns (which were the only guns used on any British tank for the first two and a half years of the War) were woefully inadequate weapons with which to tackle the German armoury.

The demand for tanks was of such immediacy that there was no chance of Rolls-Royce having time to design an entirely new model. They concentrated instead on fitting the Merlin engine – minus the supercharger and in this form called the Meteor – into the Crusader's existing hull. The original Crusader, although the latest tank in production in 1940, had a 330 h.p. Liberty engine which dated from the First World War; the Meteor provided 600 h.p. The difficulty of the task was still further increased by the fact that parts of the Liberty engine had been exposed on the outside of the Crusader hull and clearly such a design could not be tolerated on the new Rolls-Royce tank; the whole of the Meteor must be inside the hull under armoured protection. Somehow the Rolls-Royce team managed to do the job and in *Silver Ghosts and Silver Dawn* George Robotham, who was in charge of the project, describes the first Army trial:

> 'On the day in question I saw the course for the first time and anticipated that, with our (at that time, ungoverned) 600 h.p. engine, the Crusader might well exceed 50 m.p.h. I pointed out to the captain in charge of operations that trouble was likely to occur unless the course was altered; but he did not really understand what I was saying, and the trial proceeded according to plan . . .
>
> The Rolls-Royce-engined Crusader's appearance at maximum speed was spectacular. A plume of fine oil spray was ejected from the breather of the self-change gearbox (which as far as I know had never been run so fast before) as the eighteen tons thundered down the road. Some pedestrians halfway down the course took fright, leaped over the hedge, and ran across the fields as fast as they could . . . The little corporal who was driving must have been astounded as anyone at the speed attained but, like a good soldier, he obeyed orders and kept his foot down to the end of the straight, completely failing to round the bend. As a result the tank plunged

into the wood, decapitating a telegraph pole in the process, and distributing coils of wire in all directions. The driver was shaken but unscathed when his charger came to rest. The only indication of the speed reached was obtained from a maximum revolution recorder which we had fitted as a precaution, and which registered something in excess of 50 m.p.h. Whilst this Gilbertian sprint created great interest in the Meteor engine, it was far from solving the problem of producing a reliable 600 h.p. tank.'

In fact it was only the beginning of the problem. The instant doubling of the tank's power obviously caused all number of mechanical failures and it took forty-three days to complete the first thousand miles. The worst difficulties concerned the cooling system, and Leylands, who had been associated with Rolls-Royce in the project, despaired of ever finding a solution and pulled out. Even the discovery that the powerful fans had created such an air flow that a Leyland tester's cap had been sucked off his head, torn into shreds and plastered all over the radiators, (considerably impairing the cooling system's efficiency) did not restore Leyland's faith in the Meteor.

True to Henry Royce's principles – 'there is no such thing as an insoluble problem,' – Rolls-Royce did not despair. Lord Beaverbrook, the Minister in charge of war production, was equally confident that Rolls-Royce could overcome the difficulties and when the company asked for more money he sent the following telegram:

'Hives, Rolls-Royce, Derby. The British Government has given you an open credit for one million pounds. This is a certificate of character and reputation without precedent or equal. Beaverbrook.'

(Would Lord Beaverbrook, one wonders, have shown equal confidence in the RB. 211?) Sure enough, Rolls-Royce justified Governmental confidence and managed to devise a cooling system for the vast Meteor more efficient than that of the comparatively minute original Liberty engine.

The resulting tank was the Cromwell. Unfortunately the War Office did not match the Rolls-Royce achievement by producing adequate armaments, so that when the German Tiger tank appeared, the British were once again outgunned. Nevertheless, the Cromwell did sterling work in France and this letter from the Commander of 7th Armoured Division, Major-General G. L. Verney, quoted by W. A. Robotham, shows that Rolls-Royce's standards were as high as ever:

'I feel that I must write you a short note to tell you how superbly the Cromwell tank has been during our recent activities, and I hope that you will pass on the gist of this letter to the various people responsible for the production of this magnificent machine.

For about three weeks the Armoured Regiments have been continuously in action and the opportunities for long maintenance have been non-existent. On most days the tanks have been moving and fighting all day, going into leaguer at dark in enemy-held territory

and moving out again at dawn, which has meant that there has been
no night maintenance at all.

At dawn on August 31st we started our advance from south of
the Seine, and it has carried us 250 miles into Ghent in six days. We
have lost practically no tanks through mechanical failure (I should
say at a guess four or five per Regiment). Anyhow, so few that the
matter has been no anxiety whatever. We have had actions every
day, sometimes quite long ones and sometimes at night too, and
again during this period there has been no maintenance whatever
other than an occasional task or perhaps half an hour when there
was nothing much doing.

The tremendous speed, when the going has been good, has alone
made this great advance possible, and I wish that you and the
people who have made the tanks could have seen them tearing along
through all these French and Belgian villages. It has been a most
inspiring sight and it has thrilled the inhabitants to a really remarkable degree, especially here in Belgium.'

The Meteor engine was still being used in British tanks twenty
years later. But at the time that it was being developed Rolls-
Royce was becoming involved in another enterprise that was far
more significantly pregnant of the future. 'One day in 1942,' Sir
Frank Whittle has reported, 'Mr. Hives told me that Rolls-
Royce had decided to go all out for the gas turbine.'

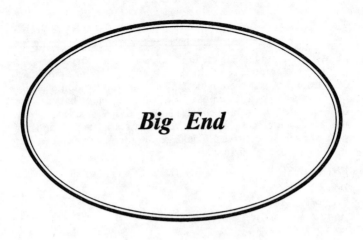

Big End

I

The first Rolls-Royce jet flew in 1943. In only a few years this new concept was to dwarf all other aspects of the company's business. There *were* other sections of Rolls-Royce – the motor car, the diesel engine, the industrial and marine gas turbine, the oil engine and small engine divisions – but these were either historical survivals or spin-offs from the huge aero-engine division. Together they contributed under 20 per cent of the company's turnover, and even less of the profit.

But the jet engine not only comprised most of the Rolls-Royce cake; it enormously inflated the cake's size. In the Sixties capital more than quadrupled, from £54 million to £223 million, and the number of employees almost doubled, reaching 87,000 (much of this huge increase being due to the Bristol Siddeley merger in 1966). Of this 87,000 payroll, 50,000 were engaged in aero-engine production and a further 18,000 on aero-engine research, design and development. In this area Rolls-Royce were, beyond dispute, the leading company in Europe, a giant among pygmies. How was it that one engine, the RB. 211, and one contract, with the American Lockheed Corporation, could bring this vast structure toppling down?

For it is immediately obvious that the advent of the jet brought no decline in the company's technical expertise. Indeed, the reverse was the case, as the briefest glance at a few of their achievements during the period under review shows. In 1953 the Flying Bedstead (or Thrust Measuring Rig in Rolls-Royce terminology) pioneered experiments in vertical take-off; the same year the Dart became the first turbo-jet in airline service; in 1958 the Comet, powered by the Avon engine, was the first jet airliner to undertake a regular transatlantic run; in 1960 the Conway was the first turbo-fan in airline service and furthermore in 1966 established a new record in being the first engine to give 10,000 hours flying time between major overhauls; in 1963 the

Spey became the first engine in airline service to carry a ten-year parts-cost guarantee. It would be labouring the point to multiply such examples, but there is no lack of material for doing so. By the middle Sixties the company was able to claim that half the civil aircraft with turbine engines sold in the West since the war had been powered by Rolls-Royce. The complete list of their post-war engine contracts would be far too long to quote, but here are some high-lights:

PRINCIPAL POST-WAR ENGINE CONTRACTS

Into *Service*	*Aircraft*
AVON TURBOJET	
1951	Canberra
1952	Vickers Swift
1952	Saab Lensen
1953	CAAC Sabre
1954	Hawker Hunter
1955	Vickers Valiant
1958	Comet IV
1958	Vickers Supermarine Scimitar
1958	Saab Draken
1959	Hawker Siddeley Sea Vixen
1959	Sud Aviation Caravelle
1960	English Electric Lightning fighters
DART TURBO-PROP	
1953	Vickers Viscount
1958	Fokker Friendship/Fairchild F.27 & FH 227
1959	Grumman Gulfstream
1961	Hawker Siddeley Argosy
1961	Handley Page Herald
1962	Hawker Siddeley 748
1965	NAMC YS 11 (Japanese)
1965	Convair 600
1966	Hawker Siddeley Andover
CONWAY TURBOFAN	
1960	Douglas DC 8
1960	Boeing 707
1961	Handley Page Victor
1964	Vickers VC 10 military transports
1965	Vickers Super VC 10 airliners
TYNE PROPJET	
1960	Vickers Vanguard
1960	Canada Yukon
1961	Canadair 44
1965	Breguet Atlantic maritime aircraft
1966	Short Belfast military transports
1968	Transall C-160 military transports

Into
Service   Aircraft

SPEY TURBOFAN
1964   Hawker Siddeley Trident
1965   BAC One-Eleven
1965   Hawker Siddeley Buccaneer S2
1966   McDonnell Phantom 2
1966   Grumman Gulfstream 2
1966   Lear Liner Model 40
1966   Fokker F28 Fellowship
1966   Hawker Siddeley HS 801

It seems unbelievable, looking at the long roll of brilliant achievement, that this triumphant story could end in tragedy. In order to explain how this did come about it is necessary to turn away briefly from Rolls-Royce and take a wider look at the problems of aero-engine manufacture in general.

The engines are the make-or-break factor in modern aircraft, the vital nucleus that controls size, performance and life span. Further, because development of an engine takes longer than that of an airframe, the engine also controls the timing of the aircraft's first appearance. Obviously the aircraft manufacturers, always needing to have the edge over rivals, will particularly favour an engine that can be 'stretched' – i.e. one that can be continually developed to provide increased power and thus keep the aircraft concerned in the lead. Two examples from Rolls-Royce's experience illustrate these points particularly well.

De Havillands originally envisaged the Trident as a considerably larger plane than the one that was actually produced. The first plans were for a plane similar to the Boeing 727 which later became a tremendous international success when America took up the idea of a three-engined airliner. Rolls-Royce specially developed the Medway for Trident. At the last moment, however, B.E.A. rejected the Medway-powered Trident as too big, and scaled down the whole project to the 100-passenger aircraft which in fact came into service in 1964. This has proved a mistake, for the Trident, unlike the Boeing 727, has not been an outstanding commercial success. One of the reasons for this failure was that the Spey, the engine which Rolls-Royce provided for the production Trident after the rejection of the Medway, could not be stretched enough to boost the Trident's performance and capacity into the market which Boeing cornered.

The European airbus provides the second example, this time of the size of a plane being scaled upwards by the choice of engine. In the first outline plans of 1965 the airbus was to be a medium-sized aircraft by contemporary standards, with a capacity of about 200 passengers. But for external reasons, which will be investigated later, the RB. 207, a massively powerful new

Rolls-Royce engine project, was chosen to power the airbus. The RB. 207, designed as big brother to the RB. 211, tended to inflate the whole scheme, until by the end of 1967 the airbus had mushroomed to a proposed 300-seat aircraft. At this stage it would have been competing in the Jumbo-jet market, without the advantages of the Jumbo's range. So the first European airbus, the A.300, was abandoned; the designers went back to their boards and produced the A.300 B.

These illustrations demonstrate how important it is for aircraft manufacturers to choose the right engine at the right time. And their need to keep ahead in the cut-throat competition for orders means that there is an ever-pressing demand for new engines, particularly engines that will 'stretch'. As the inevitable result of these pressures, an engine's life, for all the millions lavished on its development, is relatively very short, perhaps a decade at most. To recoup costs it must sell in large numbers during that time.

Moreover, the aero-engine companies are under pressure from within as well as from without. The development and production of a successful engine expands a company's resources, both of manpower and capital. There must be orders for the next generation of engines to take up these resources. One technical triumph voraciously demands another. If Rolls-Royce were to survive, they had to press onwards.

At this point one must outline the most important stages in the development of the jet engine. The basic principle on which all jet engines operate is that turbine blades force air into a combustion chamber where fuel is ignited so that the escaping gases produce a direct thrust at the rear of the engine, while at the same time driving the central turbine shaft. There have been three important modifications to this basic principle:

1. The turbo-prop (e.g. the Dart): Here the name is self-explanatory; the central shaft of the turbine drives a propeller at the front and the thrust of the jet is used only indirectly.

2. The turbo-fan (e.g. the Spey): Turbo-fan engines power most of the aircraft now operating. In this case the thrust is used directly, but there are two shafts, one carrying the high pressure turbine blades and the other a series of slower speed fans at the front of the engine. These fans take part of the air round the outside of the combustion chamber, though still inside the engine. This 'by-pass' air cools the inner jet.

3. The three-shaft 'advanced technology' fan engine (e.g. the RB. 211): This engine has three shafts. The innermost carries a large enclosed fan at the front of the engine, while the other two drive high pressure turbines in a manner similar to the ordinary turbo-fan engine. Much of the air from the main fan provides direct thrust not passing through the rest of the engine at all.

To aero-engine companies these developments have presented

hurdles of successively increasing height, not only in technology but also in economics. The costs of research and development have mushroomed astoundingly. The final estimates for bringing the RB. 211 into production were in the region of £170 million, compared with which the development cost of the Spey seems chicken-feed at around £20 million. Yet if the penalty of failing these hurdles was bankruptcy, the penalty of not tackling them was insignificance. It was unthinkable that Rolls-Royce, whose whole history consisted of successful response to technological challenge and who knew that such challenge was a prerequisite of technological advance, should ever pull up short. Naturally they led the field.

This response was the more certain because almost to the end engineers were predominant in the company's boardroom. 'A basic engineering training is a good training for management and for top engineering decisions.' Such a statement encapsulates the Rolls-Royce philosophy. And it came from a man whose own background was right in the Royce tradition. Sir Denning Pearson had achieved a first class engineering degree from spare-time study while working in a shipyard. He owed this break-through into top management to Lord Hives who had sent him to Canada to sell the Merlin immediately after the war. Hives had begun working under Royce so the line of succession was unbroken. Before Rolls-Royce merged with Bristol Siddeley in 1966 only one of their eight directors had been with them for less than twenty-five years. Such links with the past were to be found on every level: In 1964 over a third of the workers in the Derby factory had been employed there since before the Second World War.

It is nowadays the fashion to consider 'management' as a special art, distinct, esoteric and above all serious, quite beyond the reach of those who have not given a slice of their youth to (preferably American) business schools. There has been no lack of management consultants averring that the Rolls-Royce debacle was due to lack of management consultants. And, following this trend, some of the press have castigated the company for its 'arrogance' in presuming to attempt stiff technological hurdles on slender resources. But if the company was arrogant, it was, as we have seen, an enforced arrogance. Moreover for years before the crash the press had been applauding a series of brilliant successes achieved by this same engineering management. The Dart (turbo-prop) and the Spey (turbo-fan) hurdles had presented exactly that same kind of difficulty to the company as did the RB. 211, though on a far smaller scale. On the first two Rolls-Royce took the necessary gamble and won; on the third the dice were loaded against them.

After the war there had been endless problems in the develop-ment of the Dart turbo-prop, and Rolls-Royce encountered much criticism over the project. The Dart had been designed to

weigh 600 lb. and to produce a 1000 lb. thrust, but the first prototype emerged with these figures reversed: weight 1000 lb. and
thrust 600 lb. In the true Royce tradition, the company stuck to
its task of ironing out the difficulties, and managed to get back
to the design figures. Vickers, who throughout all troubles over
the Dart had kept their faith in Rolls-Royce, were eventually
rewarded with an engine so far ahead of its competitors that
they were able to produce the first turbo-prop plane to go into
regular airline service. This was the Viscount and it became
Britain's best selling plane since the war; nearly 450 have been
exported. The Dart, 'the Volkswagen of the air', was remarkable
for its reliability and endurance.

Moving on to turbo-fan engines, the origin of the Spey again
illustrates the company's ability boldly to gamble its way out of
a corner. This time, as we have already seen, the difficulty came
from outside. BEA's last-moment decision to scale down the
Trident and the consequent abandonment of the Medway cost
Rolls-Royce £4¼ million. Undeterred, the company immediately
invested £20 million of its own resources in a new engine, the
Spey. As Sir Denning Pearson said: 'If we'd been run by accountants we'd never have gone ahead with the Spey.' Once again,
however, the gamble succeeded. Though Trident was not a
success, the Spey engine found military outlets, in the Phantom
and the Buccaneer.

So, in 1970, the Chairman could claim in his annual statement
that while the government had invested £33·6 million in the
launching programmes for Dart, Avon, Conway and Spey, Rolls-
Royce had contributed just over £90 million of its own funds.
Total business from these engines was estimated at £1,260
million, 75 per cent for export. The government had more than
recovered its investment in the Dart and seemed likely to recover
its total investment in the other three engines before they went
out of service.

By 1970, however, Rolls-Royce were deeply in trouble with
the RB. 211 programme. This engine was to provide nearly four
times the power of the Spey, but initial estimates of development
costs (which in the event proved wildly inadequate) were, at £65
million, already three times those of Spey. Rolls-Royce had,
nevertheless, no choice but to gamble once again and produce
the engine, or one like it, if they were to stay in the big league.
Sir Denning Pearson summed it up: 'Building a new engine
would not guarantee we stayed in business. Not building one
would certainly guarantee that we went out of business.' And of
course building the engine was only the beginning; it had to be
sold. Here, as will now be explained, Rolls-Royce were competing
under a handicap.

II

Air transport has been an outstanding growth industry of the post-war era. In the 1960s passenger traffic increased at an average rate of 13·7 per cent per year and cargo at an even greater pace. The 1970s were expected to see orders for Concorde, the Boeing 747, the Lockheed L.1011, the McDonnell Douglas DC 10 and the European Airbus to the tune of some £14,000 million.

That sounds like a good business in which to be involved. This huge market is dominated, however, by the United States, both as customer and as producer; America makes 70 per cent of all airframes in the western world. The basis of this dominance is that huge government defence contracts guarantee the American aircraft industry production runs long enough to recoup the costs of research and development. 'Guarantee' is the precise term, for 'Buy American' rules forbid the United States government to obtain military supplies from abroad unless the alien product is at least 50 per cent cheaper. (The recent sale of the Harrier vertical take-off fighter is an isolated exception, made under the terms of the offset agreement resulting from the cancellation of the F.111). So in practice the American aircraft industry obtains sole benefit from these contracts and a British company like Rolls-Royce is virtually excluded from the biggest and safest market in the world. In 1970 the United States government spent £3,800 million on aerospace products. In addition the Pentagon laid out a further £3,100 million on research and development, some of it of benefit to the industry. And on top even of these vast sums American aerospace concerns drew an average of £1,600 million a year from the 1960s space programme. As the Vietnam war winds down government contracts become worth rather less, but the effects of this decline take time to be felt.

Although the civil market in America is far more accessible the advantages of military research and development can obviously be carried over into the civil field. An engine developed for a military plane may well find a civil application. Further, as the background to the Lockheed/Rolls-Royce contract demonstrated, there are strong political pressures, even if no actual legislation, pushing American companies into buying home products. There has also been a 10 per cent import duty on aero-engines. Altogether if Rolls-Royce was to be competitive in the vitally important American market, it had to price its engines at least 15 per cent lower than its two giant American competitors, Pratt and Whitney and General Electric.

It is worth considering a little more closely the effect of the long production runs enjoyed by the American industry. The greater the research and development costs, the more advantageous long runs become. This point is clearly made by the

1965 Plowden report on the British aircraft industry:

> If an aircraft . . . costs £25 million to develop and £1 million each to
> produce, a manufacturer with a market of 100 could sell the aircraft
> at £1.25 million each and cover his costs; another manufacturer
> with a market of only 50 would have to charge £1.5 million each. If
> the development cost were no more than £5 million, or the total
> market sufficiently large for the sales of the two manufacturers to be
> 500 and 250 respectively, the selling price of the two aircraft would
> become £1.05 million and £1.10 million. The difference in price
> between them would then be no more than £0.05 million compared
> with £0.25 in the former example.

The Plowden report was concerned with the aircraft industry as
a whole, but of course the argument applies with equal force to
aero-engines in particular. Another factor making long runs
desirable is that the first engines, made before teething problems
have been overcome, tend to cost the manufacturer more than
the later ones. So the three-hundredth engine of a series is likely
to be more profitable than the third.

In brief their long production runs meant that the American
companies could keep their prices competitive even if their
costs were higher. This fact added further desperation to Rolls-
Royce's need to find a larger market.

Neither the British nor any other government has defence
needs remotely comparable to those of the United States. It is
true that the Korean War provided a temporary bonanza for the
British industry. But the 1957 Defence White Paper, which cut
down conventional aircraft and made the Blue Streak rocket the
keystone of our defence was a terrible blow to the industry. The
subsequent abandonment of Blue Streak was one of the first
stages in that realisation which continued to dawn throughout
the Sixties that Britain by herself could not afford high cost
advanced technology projects. Perhaps the RB.211 affair has
finally drummed this home.

The Sixties began, however, with a temporary return of hope,
false hope, to the British aircraft industry. It became clear that
the 'Doomsday-or-nothing' reliance on nuclear weapons was
inadequate as defence policy. The Government ordered a short
take-off transport, a vertical take-off fighter and the TSR 2,
hailed as one of the most formidable fighting machines in the
world. None of these orders, however, survived the financial
exigencies of the middle Sixties.

The government, recognising that the relative lack of military
orders was placing the British industry at a severe disadvantage,
has provided support for civil projects since the war, generally
seeking return from a levy on sales. Unfortunately such help has
too often been tied to the requirements of national airlines
instead of being given to projects which meet the demands of the
international market. In 1965 the only civil ventures which had

shown profit for the government were the Viscount and the Dart
engine. Obviously the endless losses have tended to make the
powers-that-be less enthusiastic about propping up the aircraft
industry.

It is nonsense to blame a democratically-elected government
for showing a cheeseparing attitude. Such help could be con-
strued as a case of taxing the many to help the few, and the
aircraft industry has strong competitors for the government's
bounty. But the government *was* culpable, surely, in accompanying the necessary cancellations and caution with paeans to our
technological prowess. It was like gilding a festering lily.

Rolls-Royce have always appreciated that there was no
future in depending on the British industry alone. The only
British civil aircraft to sell in large numbers abroad since the
war have been the Viscount and the BAC 1–11: although these
successes both involved Rolls-Royce engines, they obviously did
not set the company free of the need to sell direct to foreign
aircraft manufacturers. And in fact Rolls-Royce revenue from
abroad more than doubled in the Sixties, reaching £112 million
in 1969. This compares with sales of £189 million in the United
Kingdom. Of the export sales, £54 million were to North
America, which seems a surprisingly high figure when we read
so much of Rolls-Royce wanting to break into the American
market with the RB. 211. They already had engines in American
planes. Boeing, for example, were convinced that their 707
would sell better outside America with a Rolls-Royce engine; so
the Conway powers, among others, the BOAC and the Lufthansa
707s. But what Rolls-Royce could never manage before 1968
was to persuade the American companies to instal their engines
as original equipment. Thus all Boeing 707s in the service of
American airlines, the majority by far, have Pratt and Whitney
engines.

To summarise: Rolls-Royce needed to develop the RB. 211,
or a similar engine, if they were to maintain their position as
one of the big three aero-engine manufacturers in the western
world; the enormous cost of such development demanded a
large market; and the largest market, America, was exceedingly
difficult to penetrate, owing to the inbuilt advantages enjoyed
by the American companies.

III

Faced with this dilemma, Rolls-Royce in effect had two choices.
Putting trust in their technological skills, they could aim at
producing an engine so advanced and so relatively cheap that
they would out-gun their American competitors and penetrate
the vital United States market. Or they could work with the
government for some sort of European tie-up, which would at

once provide the money for both research and development, and a market for the final product.

Unfortunately the government and Rolls-Royce opted for both these alternatives and ended with neither.

About America the company never had any doubts: 'We have to sell in America in order to live,' proclaimed Sir Denning Pearson. And another senior executive later echoed his words: 'It has been our constant and unswerving ambition to secure a major engine order in a major American airframe for a major American operation.' There was always the danger that such an attitude, however well founded, would lead to disastrous under-pricing.

To the committed European salvation always seems to lie in Europe alone. Rolls-Royce have never neglected European opportunities; they have in fact been involved in several co-operative schemes. In 1960 the company signed an agreement with Motoren und Turbinen of Munich to co-operate on a jet engine development. Since 1966 Rolls-Royce and Turbomeca have been jointly producing the Adour engine for the Anglo-French strike trainer aircraft. The Olympus 593 engine has been developed with the nationalised French SNECMA concern to power the Concorde. Most important of all, in 1969 Rolls-Royce won a huge order to power the European multi-role combat aircraft (MRCA) with the RB. 199. This contract could be worth more than £600 million over the next fifteen years. But

European enthusiasts see the European airbus as Rolls-Royce's great missed opportunity in civil aviation.

The British government's involvement with the airbus began in 1965 when Roy Jenkins, a committed European, was Minister of Aviation. Britain, France and Germany were to combine to produce a big, short-to-medium-range aircraft. It was becoming clear that this type would be a leading seller in the early 1970s.

In the first plans for the airbus (the A.300), Hawker-Siddeley were to control the design of the airframe while, to keep the balance, Bristol-Siddeley were to combine with the French SNECMA to manufacture an American engine under licence. But by early 1967 the British government, seeking to protect Rolls-Royce from American competition, was exerting pressure for the adoption of a Rolls engine. France and Germany agreed, but at a price – the surrender of Hawker-Siddeley's design leadership to the French. The Rolls-Royce engine selected was the RB. 207, big brother to the RB. 211. We have already observed how this engine expanded the original A.300 airbus until by the end of 1969 it was necessary to begin again with the A.300B.

By this time Rolls-Royce had landed the Lockheed contract for the RB. 211, and therefore no longer felt the same pressing need to sell the RB. 207 in Europe. At the same time the French rightly began to doubt Rolls-Royce's capacity to develop two advanced-technology engines at the same time. This doubt was

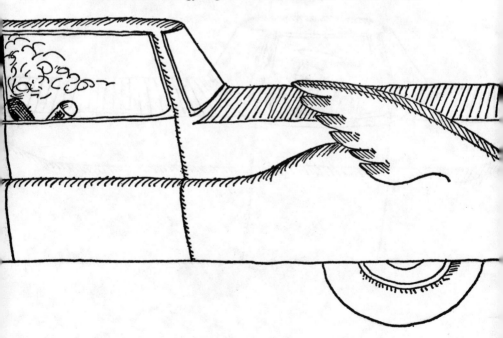

confirmed when Rolls-Royce sought to foist the RB. 211, in an
up-rated version, onto the European airbus scheme. To our
European partners it must have seemed that the only consistent
principle in Britain's policy was that the airbus should have a
Rolls-Royce engine; exactly which engine appeared to be of
secondary importance.

It was in fact all too obvious that both Rolls-Royce and the
government, having obtained the American contract, were
putting the United States first and just stringing Europe along.
This was confirmed when in March 1969 the British government
pulled out of the airbus project, pleading, in the execrable
jargon of the age, that its 'cost-benefit analysis' showed that the
airbus was not a paying proposition. It is true that the estimated
costs were high; more rarely, they may also have been accurate.
Shortly after, the remaining European partners decided on an
American engine for the A.300B. Britain's failure clearly to
define objectives and stick to one policy had ended in disaster.

Hindsight suggests that Rolls-Royce may have been mistaken
in concentrating on selling in America instead of committing
themselves wholeheartedly to the European alternative. Yet at
the time there was never enough certainty that the airbus
project would get off the ground for Rolls-Royce to depend on
it entirely. Part of this uncertainty, it is true, was of their own
making; but the fact that there were no firm orders for the
A.300B in 1969 would have made involvement in this aircraft's

future a hazardous gamble.

If European co-operation over aircraft is to succeed, there must be a more efficient mechanism for liaison than simple government-to-government collaboration. Where a number of separate companies are involved, it is difficult to establish a tight central control over spending. The history of Concorde's soaring costs makes clear the disastrous effects of such a difficulty. Estimates for Concorde's development rose from £140 million in 1962 to £730 million in 1970 and are still rising. But where one international company has been formed to develop an aircraft, like Turbo-Union in the case of the European MRCA, the check on costs has been more efficient. It is arguable that a nationalised Rolls-Royce will find it easier to combine with European aero-engine companies (most of which are also nationalised) in this manner than the old private company, which naturally tended to attach itself to individualist traditions. Further, the European companies will no longer need to fear being dwarfed by the Rolls-Royce giant.

This consideration of the European alternative, however, has taken the narrative too far ahead. Before 1968 Rolls-Royce had proclaimed their intention of making a decisive breakthrough into the American civil aviation market. Throughout the 1960s they fought towards this goal. They tried hard, for example, to get their engines into the Boeing 707 and later into the Boeing Jumbo. Although in both cases the Rolls-Royce tender was

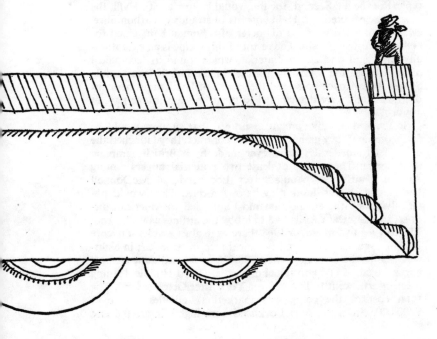

cheaper (even after allowing for import duty) and in the latter case their proffered engine was technologically more advanced than those of American rivals, they failed to win either of these two contracts. Instead of damping their enthusiasm, these reverses redoubled it. And in the RB. 211 they finally believed that they had found a winner.

Even the Americans were inclined to concede in 1967/68 that the RB. 211 was two years ahead of any competitor. At the planning stages the engine appeared to be an airframe manufacturer's dream. It would be colossally powerful, producing a 40,000 lb. thrust even in its initial version. Because it would run at a low temperature there was tremendous stretch potential, up to at least a 55,000 lb. thrust. (The Spey has a maximum thrust of 15,000 lb. and the thrust of the Welland, Rolls-Royce's first production jet engine, was only 1,500 lb.). Notwithstanding such power the RB. 211 would be relatively lighter, cheaper to run, simpler in construction (with 40 per cent fewer component parts), and easier to maintain than existing turbo-fan engines. Moreover, in a world increasingly environment-conscious, it would be quieter. The new engine owed these assets to two main factors. First, the huge fan (about eight feet in diameter) would be driven and controlled independently: this would mean that it could be slowed down, thus reducing noise, during the landing approach and immediately after take-off. The elimination of guide vanes ahead of the fan would also cut out the high-pitched scream typical of the jet. Second, the fan would be made with Hyfil, the new miracle ingredient. Hyfil consists of strands of carbon fibre, each about a tenth of the diameter of a human hair, glued together by a strong resin. The result of this recipe is an exceptionally stiff, light and cheap material, which found its 'ecological niche' (to use the scientists' phrase) in the fan. In the middle Sixties Rolls-Royce possessed the secrets of Hyfil, the Americans did not. Rolls were determined to make this advantage pay, at any cost.

So, backed by government assurance that support would be forthcoming if they gained a suitable contract, they launched the most determined sales drive ever made by a British company in America. There were at least two potential buyers among American airframe manufacturers, Lockheed and McDonnell Douglas: each was developing its own airbus. They would obviously install the engine that most appealed to American airlines, so that meant Rolls had to lobby the airlines as well. From March 1966 to September 1968 there were always at least twenty Rolls-Royce marketing and technical men in America; in eighteen months the company spent £80,000 on transatlantic airfares and a further £6,000 on telephone calls. David Huddie, leading these efforts, went to live in New York after October 1967. The total cost of the company's marketing activities was over £400,000. From the start Lockheed were highly interested and

Rolls-Royce cut their prices to sustain that interest. The Americans of course calculated on Rolls' determination to land a contract and held out for even lower prices before committing themselves. In their fervour Rolls-Royce did not, could not, assess the danger in thus whittling away their profit margins. In November 1967 devaluation gave them the opportunity for a five per cent cut in their price. At this stage the RB. 211 cost $508,000, the General Electric rival engine $630,000 and Pratt and Whitney's $700,000. In February 1968, General Electric, alarmed by the lead Rolls appeared to have, brought their price down to $600,000; Rolls-Royce immediately countered by lowering theirs still further to $485,000.

It was crazy, but it achieved its ill-starred objective. Quite early Lockheed had decided that they wanted the engine. The difficulty was that a huge order to Rolls-Royce would be a severe blow to the American balance of payments, then deteriorating badly. No American airline could get away with offending the government and antagonising public opinion by a callous disregard of the needs of the U.S. economy. Lockheed therefore initiated an offset arrangement: an English company, Air Holdings, would buy fifty of the completed airbuses thus restoring to the United States what Rolls-Royce would milk away.

With this agreement pending, General Electric knew that they were losing the battle. (Pratt and Whitney had dropped out of the race in December 1968). They therefore played their last card and called in the politicians. Senator Lausche and Representative Robert Taft Jr., both from Ohio where General Electric manufactured their engines, marshalled the arguments: a deal with Rolls-Royce would do $3,800 million damage to the United States balance of payments and cost Ohio 10,000 jobs. Worse, the deal was, they urged, un-American; Rolls-Royce were government-supported and therefore the competition was unfair. This last argument must have seemed particularly ironic to Rolls-Royce whose position had ever since the war been threatened by the advantages their American rivals drew from government defence contracts. But Mr. Taft knew only the outrage of the righteous.

With the offset deal in hand, the U.S. government could afford to disregard his fulminations. Meanwhile, American Airlines had ordered the McDonnell Douglas airframe, postponing a decision about the engine. (They eventually decided on General Electric). This was a blow to Lockheed but in the Rolls-Royce engine and the offset agreement they had assets sufficient to render their airframe attractive to other airlines. On 29 March 1968 a tripartite deal involving Lockheed, Rolls-Royce and three airlines was announced. Eastern Airways ordered fifty, Trans World Airlines forty-four and Air Holdings (the U.K. company) fifty of the Lockheed L.1011 airbus. The contract was worth about a million pounds on each of the three-engined aircraft to Rolls-Royce who

would receive £150 million from these initial orders. There was
talk of Rolls-Royce amassing a total of £1,000 million from possible future sales of the airbus.

With the benefit of hindsight it now seems extraordinary to recall the rapture with which the news of the contract was received
by press and politicians in Britain. It appeared as the first economic good tidings since the pound's devaluation in November
1967. Those were the days when, inspired by Mr. Robert Max-
well, we were all supposedly backing Britain. In fact the British
public, having understandably rejected Mr. Macmillan's suggestion that exporting was fun, seemed to have reluctantly resigned
itself to the alternative Wilsonian doctrine that it was a patriotic
duty laid upon the purposive. The Minister of Technology's
vocabulary struggled to whip us into euphoric frenzy that would
match the hour: the contract was, Mr. Wedgwood Benn said,
'a terrific boost to British technology and its export potential'. It certainly seemed to be a terrific boost to Mr. Benn.
Editorial after editorial gave vent to panegyrics on our technological might. One distinguished paper explained that Rolls-
Royce's success was due to careful control of costs – 'value
engineering' was the name that graced this form of thrift – and
expatiated on the vital part the company's computer centre had
played in the process. The trouble was, however, that Rolls-
Royce had not cut their costs; they had cut their prices, a very
different procedure, which does not require a computer.

Of course the public had no means of appreciating this distinc-
tion at the time, but what is more surprising is that the management of Rolls-Royce themselves gave no sign of realising that the
ground on which they stood acknowledging the plaudits was
dangerously unsure. Perhaps those computers obscured the facts;
at all events Sir Denning Pearson's comments were akin to Mr.
Wedgwood Benn's:

> 'The outcome of this hard-fought sales campaign confirms the
> ability of a technologically-based British industry to expand its
> penetration of the United States market.'

He caught the contemporary mood exactly: theirs was not to
count the cost, theirs was but to export and die. For though the
public were applauding a triumph Rolls-Royce's head had been
forced into a noose.

IV

For the contract which Rolls-Royce had signed was just that.
Lockheed meant to leave nothing to chance and the document
ran to 483 pages. But in one respect it was more remarkable for
what it lacked than for what it contained. There was no sufficient
provision made for the effect of inflation; the complicated for-

mula devised to cover this proved woefully inadequate to Rolls-Royce. But the contract did contain savage penalty clauses which guaranteed Lockheed huge sums in the event of late delivery. And the time limits fixed were exceptionally short, the whole contract being due to be completed by November 1971. It seemed to ensure that, whatever Rolls-Royce's difficulties, Lockheed would survive.

Rolls-Royce could only have accepted such terms in the hope that this original contract would prove a preliminary to further, more advantageous orders. Meanwhile, their hopes could only be for survival. This they could achieve if development of the RB. 211 encountered no problems and their cost estimates proved accurate. Otherwise the alternatives the contract presented were huge government loans, or, if these were not forthcoming, bankruptcy.

The government was committed to providing aid for research and development. The first estimates were that the cost would be £65 million, and almost immediately Mr. Wedgwood Benn made available £47 million. But very soon it was evident that, despite the computers and the 'value engineering', Rolls-Royce's calculations had been wildly inaccurate. Even in 1968 there were whispers that the company was in grave trouble. The share price, which had risen nearly twenty per cent on the day of the contract's announcement, began its steady downward drift. For, in order to pay for the RB. 211's development, Rolls-Royce were being forced to perilous financial procedures.

Even when developing the Spey it had been impossible to provide the funds required out of the profit and loss account. Rolls-Royce therefore treated as capital expenditure such development costs as would be recoverable from existing orders for the Spey. It would be written off as the money from these orders began to flow in. Rolls-Royce thus avoided a series of annual losses that would have alarmed the shareholders and made further capital impossible to raise. In the case of the RB. 211, however, they carried this procedure a dangerous step further. Now they capitalised launching costs not just to the extent of existing orders but according to their *estimates* of what future orders might be. Of course there was always the temptation to bump up these estimates.

This was becoming increasingly often. From the start Rolls-Royce were spending on the RB. 211 at double the anticipated rate. One reason for soaring costs was that Hyfil, the carbon fibre compound of which the huge fan was made, proved unable to stand up to all the necessary tests. Jet engines tend to suck in all objects in their vicinity, from birds to hailstones. (The R.A.F. loses about £1 million per year from birdstrikes.) Unfortunately Rolls-Royce found that when they fired flocks of 'pseudo birds' at 1,000 m.p.h. into the engine during trials the Hyfil fan tended to shred at the leading edges. The fibre was reinforced with steel but this in turn created stresses at the root of the blade. Given time, scientists were confident of overcoming these problems but the airlines insisted, as prospective customers, that Rolls-Royce, to insure against the failure of Hyfil, should also develop the engine with titanium blades. But titanium added 300 lb. to the engine's weight. These problems were not only exceedingly expensive, they also delayed the RB. 211's production, thus bringing Rolls-Royce into the ambit of the penalty clauses. Another factor which multiplied costs was that such a vast engine demanded entirely new testing facilities; for example Rolls-Royce had to spend millions of pounds designing and producing apparatus to test the engine in high cross-winds.

Compared with such outlay, the efforts which the company made at economy were like trying to empty the ocean with a tea-spoon. Over 3,000 men were laid off aero-engine production. Even the tiniest economies were not neglected: neither the company magazines nor the canteen service were spared. Moreover, it would be entirely unjust to blame the unions for Rolls-Royce's troubles. As in nearly all big companies at the time there were continual wage demands and a few strikes, but the rising price of labour accounted for only about fifteen per cent of the RB. 211's increased costs which by 1970 were more than double the original estimate. The outlook was the bleaker because Lockheed had not managed to make many further sales of the airbus; by February 1971 they had orders for a total of only about 180.

It was clear that only two things could save Rolls-Royce. Either they must renegotiate the contract with Lockheed, or the government must advance further massive loans.

Lockheed had their own difficulties, having suffered a $200 million loss on a contract with the American government. They could not afford generosity even though it was in their interest: the collapse of Rolls-Royce would prejudice the future of their airbus. Nor was the American government likely to incur odium by providing Lockheed with money that would be used to save a British firm.

The British government, however, at first seemed prepared to continue to support Rolls-Royce. In November 1970, having been informed that the development costs of the RB. 211 had now risen to £135 million, it advanced another £42 million and arranged for bank loans of a further £18 million. These advances were, however, made conditional on an accountant's review of Rolls-Royce's financial situation. Before this report appeared the company found itself short of cash even to pay its staff wages. Bankruptcy loomed.

The government was in a dilemma. The accountants soon realised that the £135 million November estimate was well short of the mark; the RB. 211 would absorb something like £170 mil-lion before it was ready to go into production. This meant that, even if the engines were delivered to Lockheed on time, Rolls-

Royce would lose £110,000 on each engine – £60 million on the whole contract. And that was not counting any of the now inevitable late-delivery penalties, which were conservatively estimated at £50 million. Altogether, if the government were to save the RB. 211, Mr. Corfield, Minister of Aviation, told the Commons on 4 February 1971, a further £150 million would be required.

In the end, the Cabinet baulked at swallowing this mammoth pill. But how to avoid it? Rolls-Royce provided engines for seventy airforces and 200 airlines; nurtured and harboured some of the country's most treasured technological expertise; employed over 80,000, and indirectly as many more in supply industries. There could be no question of allowing this vast complex of interests simply to disappear. Yet to support the company with cash would mean incurring all the obligations of the RB. 211 contract. The only way out was to allow Rolls-Royce to go bankrupt, thus effectively nullifying the obligation to Lockheed, and *then* revive the corpse minus the contract by nationalisation. It was an unattractive but economical device. (The nationalisation applied only to the aero-engine, marine and industrial gas turbine divisions of Rolls-Royce; the other divisions would be sold off privately).

Thus the company that had served its country so well was left to die for the same cause. On 4 February, 1971 Rolls-Royce declared itself bankrupt. On 23 February the new nationalised company, Rolls-Royce (1971) Ltd., took its first bow. It was 87 years since Royce set up business in Manchester and only 65 from the formation of Rolls-Royce.

A writer who has claimed the benefits of hindsight should beware of making trouble for himself with predictions. Does the future of Rolls-Royce (1971) lie in Europe? Could the company really ever return to private enterprise? Will the Royce standards still survive? What will become of the famous radiator? The questions abound, the answers are hidden. Henry Royce would have awaited the results of practical experiment. And after all, his £70 capital had not done too badly.

26 *February* 1971.

Tables

Table I ROLLS-ROYCE'S LIQUIDITY

Year	Cash, etc £000's	Bank borrowings £000's	Loans £000's
1953	225	1,586	Nil
1954	5,528	Nil	4,000
1955	2,225	102	4,000
1956	955	278	4,000
1957	2,288	477	3,997
1958	3,049	945	3,893
1959	595	1,666	3,828
1960	690	9,651	3,828
1961	455	11,668	15,663
1962	558	18,264	15,594
1963	751	11,941	15,415
1964	354	9,058	15,145
1965	386	15,311	14,867
1966	1,040	26,000	38,597
1967	710	41,284	48,572
1968	1,118	32,375	57,163
1969	848	37,027	56,650

Table II PRINCIPAL FUND-RAISING OPERATIONS

Year		Cash raised £000's
1950	1-for-3 rights issue at 75/- per share	1,437
1952	3-for-10 rights issue at 50/- per share	2,333
1954	£4m 4% Debenture stock 1974–84 at 99%	3,960
1956	1-for-6 rights issue at 77/6 per share	4,263
1957	2-for-7 rights issue at 95/- per share	10,247
1961	£12m 6½% Debenture stock 1981–86 at 99%	11,880
1966	1-for-4 rights issue at 37/- per share	11,721
1966	£10m 7¼% Debenture stock 1986–91 at 99%	9,900
1966	£20m 7¾% Debenture stock 1990–93 at par	20,000
1967	1-for-6 rights issue at 42/6 and 11-for-£150 of Convertible Loan stock	17,392
1968	£10m 8¼% Debenture stock 1990–95 at par	10,000
1968	1-for-6 rights issue at 45/- and 11-for-£150 Loan stock	21,530
1970	£10m loan from IRC at average interest rate of 7½% per annum (first tranche of a proposed £20m loan)	10,000

Table III PROFITS OF ROLLS-ROYCE

Year	Pre-tax profit £000's	Net profit £000's	Retentions £000's
1906		5	
1907		9	
1908		9	
1909		20	
1910		38	2
1911		51	2
1912		71	5
1913		91	13
1914		77	28
1915		44	32
1916		83	44
1917		142	39
1918		153	20
1919		193	7
1920		203	9
1921		107	10
1922	179	125	8
1923	157	137	10
1924	164	144	19
1925	166	141	19
1926	101	91	25
1927	157	137	30
1928	186	156	65
1929*	172	137	66
1930	117	97	65
1931	114	99	72
1932	121	106	85
1933	193	163	86
1934	262	202	73
1935	320	250	82
1936	360	270	94
1937	363	263	92
1938	450	310	96
1939	419	154	69
1940	500	200	42
1941	514	229	44
1942	556	231	48
1943	514	229	50
1944	590	240	61
1945	590	137	72
1946	677	396	169
1947	830	184	218
1948	1,002	320	194
1949	1,220	320	193
1950	1,166	363	179
1951	1,600	421	180
1952	2,211	574	273
1953	3,591	716	331

*1929 was a fourteen-month period.

Table III—*continued*

Year	Pre-tax profit £000's	Net profit £000's	Retentions £000's
1954	5,433	2,143	1,547
1955	4,644	2,129	1,503
1956	5,414	2,214	1,350
1957	5,280	2,230	1,904
1958	4,616	2,087	892
1959	4,875	2,635	1,417
1960	6,212	4,196	2,835
1961	2,544	2,544	1,531
1962	1,819	1,819	1,028
1963	5,856	4,035	2,772
1964	6,511	3,680	2,139
1965	6,933	4,554	2,863
1966	8,429	5,287	978
1967	11,827	7,252	757
1968	15,919	8,793	1,301
1969	6,407	4,135	44

First half of 1970, loss of £3m before tax

Table IV   TURNOVER IN RELATION TO RESEARCH COSTS

Year	Turnover £000's	Research & Development £000's
1956	79,872	3,006
1957	91,175	4,331
1958	95,390	5,837
1959	96,559	5,660
1960	108,347	5,358
1961	122,427	6,315
1962	109,107	4,721
1963	101,939	4,634
1964	106,392	4,565
1965	126,595	5,391
1966	170,276	6,818
1967	263,582	5,688
1968	319,536	6,364
1969	299,363	10,286

Table V WORKING CAPITAL AND ASSETS/LIABILITIES RATIO

Year	Current assets £000's	Current liabilities £000's	Ratio
1927	1,498	513	2·9
1928	1,524	474	3·2
1929	1,587	451	3·5
1930	1,540	361	4·3
1931	1,477	312	4·7
1932	1,501	311	4·8
1933	1,725	518	3·3
1934	2,032	766	2·7
1935	2,129	1,016	2·1
1936	2,250	952	2·4
1937	2,194	1,102	2·0
1938	2,696	1,439	1·9
1939	3,559	2,671	1·3
1940	4,451	3,571	1·2
1941	7,178	6,001	1·2
1942	8,169	6,899	1·2
1943	7,875	6,812	1·2
1944	8,164	6,209	1·3
1945	8,009	5,634	1·4
1946	6,644	4,459	1·5
1947	6,844	4,424	1·5
1948	6,692	3,947	1·7
1949	7,920	4,923	1·6
1950	7,261	3,977	1·8
1951	10,174	6,123	1·7
1952	14,434	8,858	1·6
1953	19,233	11,829	1·6
1954	25,871	11,725	2·2
1955	24,542	11,156	2·2
1956	31,610	14,656	2·2
1957	40,954	17,075	2·4
1958	39,760	15,354	2·6
1959	51,270	18,640	2·8
1960	65,259	33,536	1·9
1961	82,485	46,314	1·8
1962	79,798	45,766	1·7
1963	73,532	33,261	2·2
1964	80,834	33,558	2·4
1965	94,852	45,266	2·1
1966	193,679	125,938	1·5
1967	223,644	131,778	1·7
1968	234,786	121,959	1·9
1969	223,896	120,181	1·9

Table VI NET CAPITAL EMPLOYED

Year	Capital employed £000's	Bank borrowings as %	Loans as %
1953	12,191	11·5	—
1954	19,396	—	20·6
1955	19,780	0·5	20·1
1956	25,989	1·1	15·2
1957	36,879	1·3	10·7
1958	38,590	2·4	9·8
1959	44,516	3·6	8·4
1960	54,148	17·8	7·1
1961	64,650	18·0	24·2
1962	72,212	25·3	21·6
1963	70,195	17·0	22·0
1964	71,697	12·6	21·1
1965	81,408	18·8	18·3
1966	139,863	18·6	27·6
1967	188,370	21·9	25·8
1968	215,567	15·0	26·5
1969	223,087	16·6	25·4

Table VII PRIORITY PERCENTAGES

Year	% of profit absorbed by Loan capital	Ordinary dividend	Times covered
1960	2	34	3·1
1961	11	46	2·5
1962	24	56	2·4
1963	12	39	3·2
1964	13	49	2·4
1965	10	43	1·6
1966	15	84	1·0
1967	21	92	1·1
1968	19	88	1·1
1969	36	99	1·0

Table VIII GROSS TRADING REVENUE (£m)

Year	U.K.	Europe	N. America	S. America	Africa	Asia	Rest
1966	102	18	29	2	5	13	2
1967	168	29	40	6	8	9	6
1968	219	30	43	4	11	11	4
1969	189	30	54	5	8	11	4

Table IX SHARE PRICE RANGE

Year	High	Low
1960	37/6	29/7
1961	36/8	25/8
1962	31/2	17/-
1963	27/-	18/5
1964	30/10	22/1
1965	38/7	29/2
1966	51/6	37/2
1967	51/8	43/2
1968	54/10	41/-
1969	49/1	21/4
1970	25/4	7/1
1971	25/1	0/4½

Table X REVENUE FROM ABROAD

Year	£000's
1960	53,716
1961	60,174
1962	43,511
1963	38,385
1964	39,672
1965	52,862
1966	68,630
1967	97,063
1968	103,342
1969	112,063

Table XI NUMBER OF EMPLOYEES AT YEAR-END

1960	48,139 (Remuneration £36,204,000)
1961	51,918 (Remuneration £42,680,000)
1962	44,461 (Remuneration £37,397,000)
1963	43,549 (Remuneration £35,776,000)
1964	47,141 (Remuneration £43,587,000)
1965	49,698 (Remuneration £49,974,000)
1966	84,377 (Remuneration £65,889,000)
1967	88,076 (Remuneration £104,906,000)
1968	88,327 (Remuneration £111,986,000)
1969	87,097 (Remuneration £120,894,000)